W9-BCQ-554

ANALYZING THE ISSUES

CRITICAL PERSPECTIVES ON

OPIOID EPIDEMIC

Edited by Paula Johanson

Enslow Publishing

101 W. 23rd Street
Suite 240
New York, NY 10011
USA

enslow.com

Dedicated to my friend and pharmacist Leslie Keetley
"...And these two things in disease are particularly to be attended to, to do good,
and not to do harm."
Hippocrates, The History of Epidemics

Published in 2018 by Enslow Publishing, LLC
101 W. 23rd Street, Suite 240, New York, NY 10011

Library of Congress Cataloging-in-Publication Data

Names: Johanson, Paula, author.
Title: Critical perspectives on the opioid epidemic / Paula Johanson.
Description: New York : Enslow Publishing, 2018. | Series: Analyzing the issues | Includes bibliographical references and index. | Audience: Grades 7-12.
Identifiers: LCCN 2017002898 | ISBN 9780766084872 (library-bound : alk. paper)
Subjects: LCSH: Opioid abuse--United States--Juvenile literature. | Drug abuse--United States--Juvenile literature.
Classification: LCC RC568.O45.J64 2018 | DDC 362.290973--dc23
LC record available at https://lccn.loc.gov/2017002898

Printed in the United States of America

To Our Readers: We have done our best to make sure all website addresses in this book were active and appropriate when we went to press. However, the author and the publisher have no control over and assume no liability for the material available on those websites or on any websites they may link to. Any comments or suggestions can be sent by email to customerservice@enslow.com.

Excerpts and articles have been reproduced with the permission of the copyright holders.

Photo Credits: Cover, John Moore/Getty Images (activists), Thaiview/Shutterstock.com (background, pp. 4–5 background), gbreezy/Shutterstock.com (magnifying glass on spine); p. 4 Ghornstern/Shutterstock.com (header design element, chapter start background throughout book).

CONTENTS

INTRODUCTION

Opium is a resin made by the poppy flower. For thousands of years, it has been used to dull pain and relax the user. It works because the active ingredients are similar to chemicals our brains use for pain relief and for signaling among our brain cells. Opiates are medications derived from opium, such as heroin, codeine, and morphine. Synthetic opioids are similar chemically but can be derived from other sources. The word "opioid" is now used for both opiates and opioids. Because people need to be careful about becoming addicted or having a fatal overdose, many countries have laws making use of these drugs legal only under a doctor's care.

Research into the science of pain relief is ongoing. Scientists study new medications, both opioids and compounds, which work to relieve pain in different ways from opioids, either by using different chemical signals in our brains or by promoting healing of an injury. Research is also being done into other methods for relieving pain that don't use drugs. These research papers are published in peer-reviewed science journals; colleagues working in labs around the world check these conclusions and results. It is possible to consider the illegal use of opioid drugs as a very informal study of pain relief—at least, governments around the world are gathering statistics on thousands of people whose illegal use of opioid drugs has been noticed.

Unfortunately, the use of opioids is not only frowned upon by some social groups, but is also considered a horrifying crime. Many people condemn the illegal use of opioids, as well as the things some addicts do in desperation to get a dose. Some people are uncomfortable with even the medical use of such strong pain relievers. It's common for even rehabilitation clinics to consider deaths from opioid overdose to be more tragic when people became addicted to drugs that were actually prescribed. Most people consider health concerns under a doctor's care to be a legitimate need for pain relief. But when addicts are self-medicating with street drugs, the rest of society doesn't always understand what kinds of pain or misery addicts are trying to manage. Addicts don't always have tools to make better choices.

"A common theme that we see at the funeral homes is as follows: someone becomes addicted to heroin and eventually decides to get clean," writes funeral director Keith Walker. "They progress pretty well in recovery and, at some point, decide to do it again. They take the same dose as when they were regularly using, but their tolerance is now much lower, and they overdose and die. Very, very sad."[1]

In 2014, opioids killed more than 28,000 people in the United States, more than any year on record before.[2] At least half of all opioid overdose deaths involve a prescription opioid. The number of opioid overdose deaths is large. To put it in perspective, during that same year about that many people caught Lyme disease from ticks, or pertussis (whooping cough) because they hadn't been vaccinated, and more than ten times as many people in America caught gonorrhea.

This book collects articles discussing some of the perspectives people have on the opioid epidemic. Nearly all doctors and medical associations support the use of prescription opioids under a doctor's direction, and most patients try to use medication as they are told. There are also people who take opioids without consulting a doctor. Any use of opioids without great care can lead to harm and/or addiction. Some people are vulnerable to becoming addicted because of genetics or childhood experiences. There are also opportunists taking advantage of people's pain and misery to profit by aggressively marketing legal drugs from corporations or illegal drugs sold on the street.

It is hard to write anything about health care that does not make someone upset or uncomfortable. It's all right to be uncomfortable when thinking about the use or abuse of opioid drugs. Thinking about the consequences of drug use or abuse is upsetting, especially for people dealing with pain or the effects of opioids on friends or family members or in their communities.

Some of the articles reprinted in this book appeared first in electronic formats with detailed footnotes or links to websites that are mentioned in their texts. All the publications where these articles originally appeared are listed in the bibliography, and readers can find in those original publications all of those details.

CHAPTER 1

WHAT THE EXPERTS SAY

The National Institute on Drug Abuse notes, "Opioids reduce the intensity of pain signals reaching the brain and affect those brain areas controlling emotion, which diminishes the effects of a painful stimulus."[1] Through chemistry, statistics, and more, scientists study various questions on opioid addiction, including: Why are more men than women addicted? What is particularly dangerous about the drug fentanyl? Why is addiction increasing faster than the population? How is the death rate increasing among opioid users?

"Addictive tendencies arise in the parts of our brains governing some of our most basic and life-sustaining needs and functions: incentive and motivation, physical and emotional pain relief, the regulation of stress, and the capacity to feel and receive love;" Dr. Gabor Maté says about the roots of addiction in our brain neurology. "These brain circuits develop, or don't develop, largely under the influence of the nurturing environment in early life, and therefore addiction represents a failure of these crucial systems to mature in the way nature intended. The human brain continues to develop new circuitry throughout the lifespan, including well into adulthood, giving new hope for people mired in addictive patterns."[2]

This begins to explain the complexity of addiction, as well as the hope that many experts have for those who are struggling with addiction to opioids.

"OPIOID ADDICTION 2016 FACTS AND FIGURES," BY THE AMERICAN SOCIETY OF ADDICTION MEDICINE, AUGUST 2016

OPIOID ADDICTION

- Opioids are a class of drugs that include the illicit drug heroin as well as the licit prescription pain relievers oxycodone, hydrocodone, codeine, morphine, fentanyl and others.[1]
- Opioids are chemically related and interact with opioid receptors on nerve cells in the brain and nervous system to produce pleasurable effects and relieve pain.[1]
- Addiction is a primary, chronic and relapsing brain disease characterized by an individual pathologically pursuing reward and/or relief by substance use and other behaviors.[2]
- Of the 21.5 million Americans 12 or older that had a substance use disorder in 2014, 1.9 million had a substance use disorder involving prescription pain relievers and 586,000 had a substance use disorder involving heroin.[3]
- It is estimated that 23% of individuals who use heroin develop opioid addiction.[4]

NATIONAL OPIOID OVERDOSE EPIDEMIC

- Drug overdose is the leading cause of accidental death in the US, with 47,055 lethal drug overdoses in 2014. Opioid addiction is driving this epidemic, with 18,893 overdose deaths related to prescription pain relievers, and 10,574 overdose deaths related to heroin in 2014.[5]

- From 1999 to 2008, overdose death rates, sales and substance use disorder treatment admissions related to prescription pain relievers increased in parallel.[6]
- The overdose death rate in 2008 was nearly four times the 1999 rate; sales of prescription pain relievers in 2010 were four times those in 1999; and the substance use disorder treatment admission rate in 2009 was six times the 1999 rate.[7]
- In 2012, 259 million prescriptions were written for opioids, which is more than enough to give every American adult their own bottle of pills.[8]
- Four in five new heroin users started out misusing prescription painkillers.
- 94% of respondents in a 2014 survey of people in treatment for opioid addiction said they chose to use heroin because prescription opioids were "far more expensive and harder to obtain."[9]

IMPACT ON SPECIAL POPULATIONS

ADOLESCENTS (12 TO 17 YEARS OLD)

- In 2014, 467,000 adolescents were current nonmedical users of pain reliever, with 168,000 having an addiction to prescription pain relievers.[3]
- In 2014, an estimated 28,000 adolescents had used heroin in the past year, and an estimated 16,000 were current heroin users. Additionally, an estimated 18,000 adolescents had a heroin use disorder in 2014.[3]
- People often share their unused pain relievers, unaware of the dangers of nonmedical opioid use. Most adolescents who misuse prescription pain relievers are given them for free by a friend or relative.[10]

- The prescribing rates for prescription opioids among adolescents and young adults nearly doubled from 1994 to 2007.[11]

WOMEN

- Women are more likely to have chronic pain, be prescribed prescription pain relievers, be given higher doses, and use them for longer time periods than men. Women may become dependent on prescription pain relievers more quickly than men.[12]
- 48,000 women died of prescription pain reliever overdoses between 1999 and 2010.[12]
- Prescription pain reliever overdose deaths among women increased more than 400% from 1999 to 2010, compared to 237% among men.[12]
- Heroin overdose deaths among women have tripled in the last few years. From 2010 through 2013, female heroin overdoses increased from 0.4 to 1.2 per 100,000.[13]

1. How are accidental deaths from opioids a concern for anyone—or everyone—else?

2. What can large groups of people do about accidental deaths that are happening to one person at a time?

"AMERICA'S ADDICTION TO OPIOIDS: HEROIN AND PRESCRIPTION DRUG ABUSE," PRESENTED BY NORA D. VOLKOW AT THE SENATE CAUCUS ON INTERNATIONAL NARCOTICS CONTROL, FROM THE NATIONAL INSTITUTE OF DRUG ABUSE, MAY 14, 2014

[Editor's note: Figures are not included in this reprint but can be found with the original article.]

Good Morning, Madam Chair and members of the Caucus. Thank you for inviting the National Institute on Drug Abuse (NIDA), a component of the National Institutes of Health (NIH), to participate in this important hearing and contribute what I believe will be useful insights into the growing and intertwined problems of prescription pain relievers and heroin abuse in this country.

BACKGROUND

The abuse of and addiction to opioids such as heroin, morphine, and prescription pain relievers is a serious global problem that affects the health, social, and economic welfare of all societies. It is estimated that between 26.4 million and 36 million people abuse opioids worldwide,[1] with an estimated 2.1 million people in the United States suffering from substance use disorders related to prescription opioid pain relievers in 2012 and an estimated 467,000 addicted to heroin.[2] The consequences of this abuse have been devastating and are on the rise. For example, the number of unintentional overdose deaths from prescription pain relievers has soared in the United States, more than quadrupling since 1999. There is also growing evidence to suggest a relationship between increased non-medical use of opioid analgesics and heroin abuse in the United States.[3]

To address the complex problem of prescription opioid and heroin abuse in this country, we must recognize and consider the special character of this phenomenon, for we are asked not only to confront the negative and growing impact of opioid abuse on health and mortality, but also to preserve the fundamental role played by prescription opioid pain relievers in healing and reducing human suffering. That is, scientific insight must strike the right balance between providing maximum relief from suffering while minimizing associated risks and adverse effects.

ABUSE OF PRESCRIPTION OPIOIDS: SCOPE AND IMPACT

Prescription opioids are one of the three main broad categories of medications that present abuse liability, the other two being stimulants and central nervous system (CNS) depressants.

Several factors are likely to have contributed to the everity of the current prescription drug abuse problem. They include drastic increases in the number of prescriptions written and dispensed, greater social acceptability for using medications for different purposes, and aggressive marketing by pharmaceutical companies. These factors together have helped create the broad "environmental availability" of prescription medications in general and opioid analgesics in particular.

To illustrate this point, the total number of opioid pain relievers prescribed in the United States has skyrocketed in the past 25 years (**Fig. 1**).[4] The number of prescriptions for opioids (like hydrocodone and oxycodone products) have escalated from around 76 million in 1991 to nearly 207 million in 2013, with the United States their biggest consumer globally, accounting for almost 100 percent of the world total for hydrocodone (*e.g.*, Vicodin) and 81 percent for oxycodone (*e.g.*, Percocet).[5]

This greater availability of opioid (and other) prescribed drugs has been accompanied by alarming increases in the negative consequences related to their abuse.[6] For example, the estimated number of emergency department visits involving nonmedical use of opioid analgesics increased from 144,600 in 2004 to 305,900 in 2008;[7] treatment admissions for primary abuse of opiates other than heroin increased from one percent of all admissions in 1997 to five percent in 2007;[8] and overdose deaths due to prescription opioid pain relievers have more than tripled in the past 20 years, escalating to 16,651 deaths in the United States in 2010.[9]

In terms of abuse and mortality, opioids account for the greatest proportion of the prescription drug abuse problem. Deaths related to prescription opioids began rising in the early part of the 21st century. By 2002, death certificates listed opioid analgesic poisoning as a cause of death more commonly than heroin or cocaine.[10]

Because prescription opioids are similar to, and act on the same brain systems affected by, heroin and morphine (**Fig. 2**), they present an intrinsic abuse and addiction liability, particularly if they are used for non-medical purposes. They are most dangerous and addictive when taken via methods that increase their euphoric effects (the "high"), such as crushing pills and then snorting or injecting the powder, or combining the pills with alcohol or other drugs. Also, some people taking them for their intended purpose risk dangerous adverse reactions by not taking them exactly as prescribed (e.g., taking more pills at once, or taking them more frequently or combining them with medications for which they are not being properly controlled); and it is possible for a small number of people to become addicted even when they take them as prescribed, but the extent to which this happens currently is not known. It is estimated that more than 100 million people suffer from chronic pain in this country,[11] and for some of them, opioid therapy may be appropriate. The bulk of American patients who need relief from persistent, moderate-to-severe non-cancer pain have back pain conditions (approximately 38 million) or osteoarthritis (approximately 17 million).[12] Even if a small percentage of this group develops substance use disorders (a subset of those already vulnerable to developing tolerance and/ or clinically manageable physical dependence[13]), a large number of people could be affected. Scientists debate the appropriateness of chronic opioid use for these conditions in light of the fact that long-term studies demonstrating that the benefits outweigh the risks have not been conducted. In June 2012, NIH and FDA held a joint meeting on this topic,[14] and now FDA is requiring companies who manufacture long-acting and extended-release opioid formulations to conduct post-marketing research on their safety.[15]

THE EFFECTS OF OPIOID ABUSE ON THE BRAIN AND BODY

Opioids include drugs such as OxyContin and Vicodin that are mostly prescribed for the treatment of moderate to severe pain. They act by attaching to specific proteins called opioid receptors, which are found on nerve cells in the brain, spinal cord, gastrointestinal tract, and other organs in the body. When these drugs attach to their receptors, they reduce the perception of pain and can produce a sense of well-being; however, they can also produce drowsiness, mental confusion, nausea, and constipation.[16] The effects of opioids are typically mediated by specific subtypes of opioid receptors (mu, delta, and kappa) that are activated by the body's own (endogenous) opioid chemicals (endorphins, encephalins). The public health consequences of opioid pain reliever abuse are broad and disturbing. For example, abuse of prescription pain relievers by pregnant women can result in a number of problems in newborns, referred to as neonatal abstinence syndrome (NAS), which increased by almost 300 percent in the United States between 2000 and 2009. With repeated administration of opioid drugs (prescription or heroin), the production of endogenous opioids is inhibited, which accounts in part for the discomfort that ensues when the drugs are discontinued (i.e., withdrawal). Adaptations of the opioid receptors' signaling mechanism have also been shown to contribute to withdrawal symptoms.

Opioid medications can produce a sense of well-being and pleasure because these drugs affect brain regions involved in reward. People who abuse opioids may seek to intensify their experience by taking the drug in ways other than those prescribed. For example, extended-release oxycodone is designed to release slowly and steadily into the bloodstream after being taken orally in a pill; this minimizes the euphoric effects. People who abuse pills may crush them to snort or inject which not only increases the euphoria but also increases the risk for serious medical complications, such as respiratory arrest, coma, and addiction. When people tamper with long-acting or extended-release medicines, which typically contain higher doses because they are intended for release over long periods, the results can be particularly dangerous, as all of the medicine can be released at one time. Tampering with extended release and using by nasal, smoked, or intravenous routes produces risk both from the higher dose and from the quicker onset.

Opioid pain relievers are sometimes diverted for nonmedical use by patients or their friends, or sold in the street. In 2012, over five percent of the U.S. population aged 12 years or older used opioid pain relievers non-medically.[17] The public health consequences of opioid pain reliever abuse are broad and disturbing. For example, abuse of prescription pain relievers by pregnant women can result in a number of problems in newborns, referred to as neonatal abstinence syndrome (NAS), which increased by almost 300 percent in the United States between 2000 and 2009.[18] This increase is driven in part by the high rate of opioid prescriptions being given to pregnant women. In the United States, an estimated 14.4 percent of pregnant women are prescribed an opioid during their pregnancy.[19]

Prescription opioid abuse is not only costly in economic terms (it has been estimated that the nonmedical use of opioid pain relievers costs insurance companies up to $72.5 billion annually in health-care costs[20]) but may also be partly responsible for the steady upward trend in poisoning mortality. In 2010, there were 13,652 unintentional deaths from opioid pain reliever (82.8 percent of the 16,490 unintentional deaths from all prescription drugs),[21] and there was a five-fold increase in treatment admissions for prescription pain relievers between 2001 and 2011 (from 35,648 to 180,708, respectively).[22] In the same decade, there was a tripling of the prevalence of positive opioid tests among drivers who died within one hour of a crash.[23]

A property of opioid drugs is their tendency, when used repeatedly over time, to induce *tolerance*. Tolerance occurs when the person no longer responds to the drug as strongly as he or she did at first, thus necessitating a higher dose to achieve the same effect. The establishment of tolerance hinges on the ability of abused opioids (e.g., OxyContin, morphine) to desensitize the brain's own natural opioid system, making it less responsive over time.[24] This tolerance contributes to the high risk of overdose during a relapse to opioid use after a period in recovery; users who do not realize they may have lost their tolerance during a period of abstinence may initially take the high dosage that they previously had used before quitting, a dosage that produces an overdose in the person who no longer has tolerance.[25] Another contributing factor to the risk of opioid-related morbidity and mortality is the combined use of benzodiazepines (BZDs) and/or other CNS depressants, even if these agents are used appropriately. Thus, patients with chronic pain who use opioid analgesics along with BZDs (and/or alcohol) are at higher risk for overdose. Unfortunately, there are few available practice guidelines for the combined use of CNS depressants and opioid analgesics; such cases warrant much closer scrutiny and monitoring.[26] Finally, it must be noted in this context that, although more men die from drug overdoses than women, the percentage increase in deaths seen since 1999 is greater among women: Deaths from opioid pain relievers increased five-fold between 1999 and 2010 for women versus 3.6 times among men.[27]

RELATIONSHIP BETWEEN PRESCRIPTION OPIOIDS AND HEROIN ABUSE

The recent trend of a switch from prescription opioids to heroin seen in some communities in our country alerts us to the complex issues surrounding opioid addiction and the intrinsic difficulties in addressing it through any single measure such as enhanced diversion control (**Fig. 3**). Of particular concern has been the rise in new populations of heroin users, particularly young people.

The emergence of chemical tolerance toward prescribed opioids, perhaps combined in a smaller number of cases with an increasing difficulty in obtaining these medications illegally,[28] may in some instances explain the transition to abuse of heroin, which is cheaper and in some communities easier to obtain than prescription opioids.

The number of past-year heroin users in the United States nearly doubled between 2005 and 2012, from 380,000 to 670,000 (**Fig. 4**).[29] Heroin abuse, like prescription opioid abuse, is dangerous both because of the drug's addictiveness and because of the high risk for overdosing. In the case of heroin, this danger is compounded by the lack of control over the purity of the drug injected and its possible contamination with other drugs (such as fentanyl, a very potent prescription opioid that is also abused by itself).[30] All of these factors increase the risk for overdosing, since the user can never be sure of the amount of the active drug (or drugs) being taken. In 2010, there were 2,789 fatal heroin overdoses, approximately a 50 percent increase over the relatively constant level seen during the early 2000s.[31] What was once almost exclusively an urban problem is spreading to small towns and suburbs. In addition, the abuse of an opioid like heroin, which is typically injected intravenously, is also linked to the transmission of human immunodeficiency virus (HIV), hepatitis (especially Hepatitis C), sexually-transmitted infections, and other blood-borne diseases, mostly through the sharing of contaminated drug paraphernalia but also through the risky sexual behavior that drug abuse may engender.

NIDA ACTIVITIES TO STEM THE TIDE OF PRESCRIPTION OPIOID AND HEROIN ABUSE

NIDA first launched its prescription drug abuse public health initiative in 2001. Our evidence-based strategy calls for a comprehensive three-pronged approach consisting of (1) enhancing our understanding of pain and its management; (2) preventing overdose deaths; and (3) effectively treating opioid addiction.

RESEARCH ON PAIN AND NEXT GENERATION ANALGESICS.

Although opioid medications effectively treat acute pain and help relieve chronic pain for some patients,[32] their addiction risk presents a dilemma for healthcare providers who seek to relieve suffering while preventing drug abuse and addiction. Little is yet known about the risk for addiction among those being treated for chronic pain or about how basic pain mechanisms interact with prescription opioids to influence addiction potential. To better understand this, NIDA launched a research initiative on "Prescription Opioid Use and Abuse in the Treatment of Pain." This initiative encourages a multidisciplinary approach using both human and animal studies to examine factors (including pain itself) that predispose or protect against opioid abuse and addiction. Funded grants cover clinical neurobiology, genetics, molecular biology, prevention, treatment, and services research. This type of information will help develop screening and diagnostic tools that physicians can use to assess the potential for prescription drug abuse in their patients. Because opioid medications are prescribed for all ages and populations, NIDA is also encouraging research that assesses the effects of prescription opioid abuse by pregnant women, children, and adolescents, and how such abuse in these vulnerable populations might increase the lifetime risk of substance abuse and addiction.

Another important initiative pertains to the development of new approaches to treat pain. This includes research to identify new pain relievers with reduced abuse, tolerance, and dependence risk, as well as devising alternative delivery systems and formulations for existing drugs that minimize diversion and abuse (*e.g.*, by preventing tampering and/or releasing the drug over a longer period of time) and reduce the risk of overdose deaths. New compounds are being developed that exhibit novel properties as a result of their combined activity on two different opioid receptors (*i.e.*, mu and delta). Preclinical studies show that these compounds can induce strong analgesia but fail to produce tolerance or dependence. Researchers are also getting closer to developing a new generation of non–opioid-based medications for severe pain that would circumvent the brain reward pathways, thereby greatly reducing abuse potential. This includes compounds that work through a type of cannabinoid receptor found primarily in the peripheral nervous system. NIDA is also exploring the use of non-medication strategies for managing pain. An example is the use of "neurofeedback," a novel modality of the general biofeedback approach, in which patients learn to regulate specific regions in their brains by getting feedback from real-time brain images. This technique has shown promising results for altering the perception of pain in healthy adults and chronic pain patients and could even evolve into a powerful psychotherapeutic intervention capable of rescuing the circuits and behaviors impaired by addiction.

DEVELOPING MORE EFFECTIVE MEANS FOR PREVENTING OVERDOSE DEATHS

The opioid overdose antidote naloxone has reversed more than 10,000 overdose cases between 1996 and 2010, according to CDC.[33] For many years, naloxone was available only in an injectable formulation and was generally only carried by medical emergency personnel. However, FDA has recently approved a new hand-held auto-injector of naloxone to reverse opioid overdose that is *specifically designed to be given by family members or caregivers. In order to expand the options for effectively and rapidly counteracting the effects of an overdose*, NIDA is also supporting the development of a naloxone nasal spray—a needle-free, unit-dose, ready-to-use opioid overdose antidote that can easily be used by an overdose victim, a companion, or a wider range of first responders (*e.g.*, police) in the event of an emergency.[34]

RESEARCH ON THE TREATMENT OF OPIOID ADDICTION

Drug abuse treatment must address the brain changes mentioned earlier, both in the short and long term. When people addicted to opioids first quit, they undergo withdrawal symptoms, which may be severe (pain, diarrhea, nausea, vomiting, hypertension, tachycardia, seizures). Medications can be helpful in this detoxification stage, easing craving and other physical symptoms that can often trigger a relapse episode. However, this is just the first step in treatment. Medications have also become an essential component of an ongoing treatment plan, enabling opioid-addicted persons to regain control of their health and their lives.

Agonist medications developed to treat opioid addiction work through the same receptors as the addictive drug but are safer and less likely to produce the harmful behaviors that characterize addiction, because the rate at which they enter and leave the brain is slower. The three classes that have been developed to date include (1) agonists, *e.g.*, *methadone* (Dolophine or Methadose), which activate opioid receptors; (2) partial agonists, *e.g.*, *buprenorphine* (Subutex, Suboxone), which also activate opioid receptors but produce a diminished response; and (3) antagonists, *e.g. naltrexone* (Depade, Revia, Vivitrol), which block the receptor and interfere with the rewarding effects of opioids. Physicians can select from these options on the basis of a patient's specific medical needs and other factors. Research has shown methadone- and buprenorphine-containing medicines, when administered in the context of an addiction treatment program, can effectively maintain abstinence from other opioids and reduce harmful behaviors; we believe their gradual onset and long duration contribute to this ability to "stabilize" patient behavior.

Scientific research has established that medication-assisted treatment of opioid addiction is associated with decreases in the number of overdoses from heroin abuse, increases retention of patients in treatment and decreases drug use, infectious disease transmission, and criminal activity (**Fig. 5**). For example, studies among criminal offenders, many of whom enter the prison system with drug abuse problems, showed that methadone treatment begun in prison and continued in the community upon release extended the time parolees remained in treatment, reduced further drug use, and produced a three-fold reduction in criminal activity. Investment in medication-assisted treatment of opioid addiction also makes good economic sense. According to a 2005 published analysis that tracked methadone patients from age 18 to 60 and included such variables as heroin use, treatment for heroin use, criminal behavior, employment, and healthcare utilization, every dollar spent on methadone treatment yields $38 in related economic benefits—seven times more than previously thought.[36]

Buprenorphine is worth highlighting in this context for its pioneering contributions to addiction treatment. NIDA-supported basic and clinical research led to the development of this compound, which rigorous studies have shown to be effective, either alone or in combination with naloxone, in significantly reducing opiate drug abuse and cravings.

The arrival of buprenorphine represented a significant health services delivery innovation. FDA approved Subutex® (buprenorphine) and Suboxone® tablets (buprenorphine/naloxone formulation) in October 2002, making them the first medications to be eligible for prescribing under the Drug Addiction Treatment Act of 2000. Subutex contains only buprenorphine hydrochloride. This formulation was developed as the initial product. The second medication, Suboxone, contains naloxone to guard against misuse (by initiating withdrawal if the formulation is injected). Subutex and Suboxone are less tightly controlled than methadone because they have a lower potential for abuse and are less dangerous in an overdose. As patients progress in their therapy, their doctor may write a prescription for a take-home supply of the medication. To date, of the nearly 872,615 potential providers registered with the Drug Enforcement Administration (DEA), 25,021 registered physicians are authorized to prescribe these two medications. The development of buprenorphine and its authorized use in physicians' offices gives opioid-addicted patients more medical options and extends the reach of addiction medication to remote populations.

Medication-assisted treatments remain grossly underutilized in many addiction treatment settings, where stigma and negative attitudes (based on the misconception that buprenorphine or methadone "substitute a new addiction for an old one") persist among clinic staff and administrators. This leads to insufficient dosing or limitations on the duration of use of these medications (when they are used at all), which often leads to treatment failure and the perception that the drugs are ineffective, further reinforcing the negative attitudes toward their use.[37] Policy and regulatory barriers also can present obstacles.

INTEGRATING DRUG TREATMENT INTO HEALTHCARE SETTINGS

Medication-assisted treatment will be most effective when offered within the larger context of a high-quality delivery system that addresses opioid addiction not only with medication but also with behavioral interventions to support treatment participation and progress, infectious disease identification and treatment (especially HIV and HCV), screening and treatment of co-morbid psychiatric diseases, and overdose protection (naloxone). NIDA's research over the last two decades has provided us with evidence that a high quality treatment system to address opioid addiction must include all these components, yet there are currently very few systems in the United States that provide this bundle of effective services.[38] Health care reform—with a focus on both expanding access to treatment and improving the quality of care—offers hope that we may be better able to integrate drug treatment into healthcare settings and offer comprehensive treatment services for opioid addiction. We also are examining ways to use health care reform and the focus on health promotion and wellness to pay for and deliver prevention interventions targeted at children, adolescents, young adults, and high-risk adult populations like those with chronic pain or returning veterans.

PREVENTION, EDUCATION, AND OUTREACH

Because prescription drugs are safe and effective when used properly and are broadly marketed to the public, the notion that they are also harmful and addictive when abused can be a difficult one to convey. Thus, we need focused research to discover targeted communication strategies that effectively address this problem. Reaching this goal may be significantly more complex and nuanced than developing and deploying effective programs for the prevention of abuse of illegal drugs, but good prevention messages based on scientific evidence will be difficult to ignore.

Education is a critical component of any effort to curb the abuse of prescription medications and must target every segment of society, including doctors (**Fig. 6**). NIDA is advancing addiction awareness, prevention, and treatment in primary care practices, including the diagnosis of prescription drug abuse, having established four Centers of Excellence for Physician Information. Intended to serve as national models, these Centers target physicians-in-training, including medical students and resident physicians in primary care specialties (*e.g.*, internal medicine, family practice, and pediatrics). NIDA has also developed, in partnership with the Office of National Drug Control Policy (ONDCP), two online continuing medical education courses on safe prescribing for pain and managing patients who abuse prescription opioids. To date, combined, these courses have been completed over 80,000 times. Additionally, NIDA is directly reaching out to teens with its PEERx initiative, an online education program that aims to discourage prescription drug abuse among teens,[40] by providing factual information about the harmful effects of prescription drug abuse on the brain and body.

NIDA will also continue its close collaborations with ONDCP, the Substance Abuse and Mental Health Services Administration (SAMHSA), and other Federal Agencies. It will also continue to work with professional associations with a strong interest in preserving public health. For example, NIDA recently sponsored a two-day meeting in conjunction with the American Medical Association and NIH Pain Consortium, where more than 500 medical professionals, scientific researchers, and interested members of the public had a chance to dialogue about the problems of prescription opioid abuse and to learn about new areas of research. In another important collaborative effort, NIDA, CDC, SAMHSA, and the Office of the National Coordinator for Health Information Technology reviewed eight clinical practice guidelines on the use of opioids to treat pain and developed a common set of provider actions and associated recommendations.[41]

CONCLUSION

We are seeing an increase in the number of people who are dying from overdoses, predominantly after abuse of pre-scribed opioid analgesics. This disturbing trend appears to be associated with a growing number of prescriptions in and diversion from the legal market.

We commend the Caucus for recognizing the serious and growing challenge posed by the abuse of prescription and non-prescription opioids in this country, a problem that is exceedingly complex. Indeed, prescription opioids, like other prescribed medications, do present health risks but they are also powerful clinical allies. Therefore, it is imper-ative that we strive to achieve a balanced approach to ensure that people suffering from chronic pain can get the relief they need while minimizing the potential for negative consequences. We support the development and imple-mentation of multipronged, evidence-based strategies that minimize the intrinsic risks of opioid medications and make effective, long term treatments available.

1. Is it possible for a naloxone injector or inhaler for treating an opioid overdose to become as socially acceptable as an Epi-Pen, which treats an allergy emergency?

"FENTANYL LAW ENFORCEMENT SUBMISSIONS AND INCREASES IN SYNTHETIC OPIOID–INVOLVED OVERDOSE DEATHS – 27 STATES, 2013–2014," BY R. MATTHEW GLADDEN, PEDRO MARTINEZ, AND PUJA SETH, FROM *MORBIDITY AND MORTALITY WEEKLY REPORT*, AUGUST 26, 2016

[*Editor's note: Figures and tables are not included in this reprint and can be found with the original article.*]

In March and October 2015, the Drug Enforcement Administration (DEA) and CDC, respectively, issued nationwide alerts identifying illicitly manufactured fentanyl (IMF) as a threat to public health and safety *(1,2)*. IMF is unlawfully produced fentanyl, obtained through illicit drug markets, includes fentanyl analogs, and is commonly mixed with or sold as heroin *(1,3,4)*. Starting in 2013, the production and distribution of IMF increased to unprecedented levels, fueled by increases in the global supply, processing, and distribution of fentanyl and fentanyl-precursor chemicals by criminal organizations *(3)*. Fentanyl is a synthetic opioid 50–100 times more potent than morphine *(2)*.* Multiple states have reported increases in fentanyl-involved overdose (poisoning) deaths (fentanyl deaths) (2). This report examined the number of drug products obtained by law enforcement that tested positive for fentanyl (fentanyl submissions) and synthetic opioid–involved deaths other than methadone (synthetic opioid deaths), which include fentanyl deaths and deaths involving other synthetic opioids (e.g., tramadol). Fentanyl deaths are not reported separately in national data. Analyses also were conducted on data from 27 states[†] with consistent death certificate reporting of the drugs involved in overdoses. Nationally, the number of fentanyl submissions and synthetic opioid deaths increased by 426% and 79%, respectively, during 2013–2014; among the 27 analyzed states, fentanyl submission increases were strongly correlated with increases in synthetic opioid deaths. Changes in fentanyl submissions and synthetic opioid deaths were not correlated with changes in fentanyl prescribing rates, and increases in fentanyl submissions and synthetic opioid deaths were primarily concentrated in eight states (high-burden states). Reports from six of the eight high-burden states indicated that fentanyl-involved overdose deaths were primarily driving increases in synthetic opioid deaths. Increases in synthetic opioid deaths among high-burden states disproportionately involved persons aged 15–44 years and males, a pattern consistent with previously documented IMF-involved deaths (5). These findings, combined with the approximate doubling in fentanyl submissions during 2014–2015 (from 5,343 to 13,882) (6), underscore the urgent need for a collaborative public health and law enforcement response.

Data were analyzed from four sources: 1) fentanyl submission data from the DEA National Forensic Laboratory

Information System (NFLIS), which systematically collects drug identification results from drug cases submitted for analysis to forensic laboratories[§]; 2) synthetic opioid deaths, calculated using the National Vital Statistics System multiple cause-of-death mortality files[¶]; 3) national and state fentanyl prescription data that are estimated from IMS Health's National Prescription Audit collecting 87% of retail prescriptions in the United States[**]; and 4) medical examiner/coroner reports or death certificate data from states with a high burden of synthetic opioid deaths (i.e., a 1-year increase in synthetic opioid deaths exceeding two per 100,000 residents, or a 1-year increase of ≥100 synthetic opioid deaths during 2013–2014). Synthetic opioid deaths were identified using the following *International Classification of Diseases, 10th Revision* codes: 1) an underlying cause-of-death code of X40–44 (unintentional), X60–64 (suicide), X85 (homicide), or Y10–Y14 (undetermined intent) and 2) a multiple cause-of-death code of T40.4. In 2014, any information on the specific drug or drugs involved in a drug overdose were reported for approximately 80% of drug overdose deaths; this proportion varied over time and by state *(7)*. State analyses were limited to 27 states meeting the following criteria: 1) >70% of drug overdose deaths reported at least one specific drug in 2013 and 2014; 2) the change in the percentage of overdose deaths reporting at least one specific drug from 2013 to 2014 was <10%;[††] 3) ≥20 synthetic opioid deaths occurred during 2013 and 2014; and 4) fentanyl submissions were reported in 2013 and 2014. [§§] These 27 states accounted for 75% of synthetic opioid deaths in the United States in 2014. Analyses compared changes in the crude rate of fentanyl submissions, fentanyl prescriptions, and synthetic opioid deaths during 2013–2014 using Pearson correlations.

States were classified as high-burden if they experienced a 1-year increase in synthetic opioid deaths exceeding two per 100,000 residents or a 1-year increase of ≥100 synthetic opioid deaths during 2013–2014. Additional evidence from published state medical examiner/coroner or death certificate reports was reviewed to understand whether increases in synthetic opioid deaths were being primarily driven by fentanyl deaths and not by other synthetic opioids. Demographic characteristics of synthetic opioid deaths for high-burden and low-burden states were described.

During 2013–2014, fentanyl submissions in the United States increased by 426%, from 1,015 in 2013 to 5,343 in 2014, and synthetic opioid deaths increased by 79%, from 3,105 in 2013 to 5,544 in 2014. [¶¶] In contrast, fentanyl prescription rates remained relatively stable (Figure 1). Although changes in fentanyl submissions and synthetic opioid death rates from 2013–2014 among the 27 states were highly correlated (r = 0.95) (Figure 2), changes in state-level synthetic opioid deaths were not correlated with changes in fentanyl prescribing (data not shown). During 2013–2014, the synthetic opioid crude death rate in the eight high-burden states increased 174%, from 1.3 to 3.6 per 100,000 (Table), and the fentanyl submissions rate increased by 1,000% from 0.5 to 5.5 per 100,000. Six of the eight high-burden states reported increases in synthetic opioid death rates exceeding 2.0 per 100,000 population, and seven states reported increases in deaths of ≥100. [***] The eight high-burden states were located in the Northeast (Massachusetts, Maine, and New Hampshire), Midwest (Ohio), and South (Florida, Kentucky, Maryland, and North Carolina). Six of the eight states published data on fentanyl deaths from 2013 and 2014. [†††] Combining results across the state reports, total fentanyl deaths during 2013–2014 increased by 1,008, from 392 (2013) to 1,400 (2014), and the increase in total fentanyl deaths was of nearly the same magnitude as the increase in 966 synthetic opioid deaths in these states (589 [2013], 1,555 [2014]). This finding indicates that increases in fentanyl deaths were driving the increases in synthetic opioid deaths in these six states. Among high-burden states, all demographic groups experienced substantial increases in synthetic opioid death rates. Increases of >200% occurred among males (227%); persons aged 15–24 years (347%), 25–34 years (248%), and 35–44 (230%)[§§§] years; Hispanics (290%), and persons living in large fringe metro areas (230%). The highest rates of synthetic opioid deaths in 2014 were among males (5.1 per 100,000); non-Hispanics whites (4.6 per 100,000); and persons aged 25–34 years (8.3 per 100,000), 35–44 years (7.4 per 100,000), and 45–54 years (5.7 per 100,000) (Table).

DISCUSSION

In the 27 states meeting analysis criteria, synthetic opioid deaths sharply increased in the eight high-burden states, and complementary data suggest this increase can be attributed to fentanyl. Six of the eight high-burden states reported substantial increases in fentanyl deaths during 2013–2014, based on medical examiner/coroner data or literal text searches of death certificates. The high potency of fentanyl and the possibility of rapid death after fentanyl administration *(8)*, coupled with the extremely sharp 1-year increase in fentanyl deaths in high-burden states, highlights the need to understand the factors driving this increase.

IMF production and distribution began increasing in 2013 and has grown to unprecedented levels in 2016 *(3)*.

For example, there were approximately eight times as many fentanyl submissions in 2015 as there were in 2006 during the last multistate outbreak involving IMF *(3)*. DEA has not reported a sharp increase in pharmaceutical fentanyl being diverted from legitimate medical use to illegal uses *(4)*. Given the strong correlation between increases in fentanyl submissions (primarily driven by IMF) *(3,4)* and increases in synthetic opioid deaths (primarily fentanyl deaths), and uncorrelated stable fentanyl prescription rates, it is hypothesized that IMF is driving the increases in fentanyl deaths. Findings from DEA *(3,4)*, state, and CDC *(5)* investigations documenting the role of IMF in the observed increases in fentanyl deaths further support this hypothesis. The demographics of synthetic opioid deaths are rapidly changing and are consistent with the changes in demographics of persons using heroin, in particular, increasing use among non-Hispanic white men aged 25–44 years *(9)*. Historically, the heroin market in the United States has been divided along the Mississippi River, with Mexican black tar and brown powder heroin being sold in the west and white powder heroin being sold in the east. IMF is most commonly mixed with or sold as white powder heroin *(4)*. The concentration of high-burden states east of the Mississippi River is consistent with reports of IMF distribution in white powder heroin markets *(3,4)*.

An urgent, collaborative public health and law enforcement response is needed to address the increasing problem of IMF and fentanyl deaths *(6)*. Recently released fentanyl submissions data indicate that 15 states experienced >100 fentanyl submissions in 2015. This is up from 11 states in 2014. The national increase of 8,539 in fentanyl submissions from 2014 (5,343) to 2015 (13,882) *(6)*exceeded the increase of 4,328 from 2013 to 2014. This finding coupled with the strong correlation between fentanyl submissions and fentanyl-involved overdose deaths observed in Ohio and Florida *(5)* and supported by this report likely indicate the problem of IMF is rapidly expanding. Recent (2016) seizures of large numbers of counterfeit pills containing IMF indicate that states where persons commonly use diverted prescription pills, including opioid pain relievers, might begin to experience increases in fentanyl deaths *(3)* because many counterfeit pills are deceptively sold as and hard to distinguish from diverted opioid pain relievers. Finally, the approximate tripling of heroin-involved over-dose deaths since 2010 highlights the need for interventions targeting the illicit opioid market.[¶¶¶]

The findings in this report are subject to at least four limitations. First, national vital statistics data only report synthetic opioid deaths. A review of state-level reports in six of eight high-burden states indicated that the increase in fentanyl deaths was the primary factor driving increases in synthetic opioid deaths during 2013–2014. Because synthetic opioid deaths include deaths involving synthetic opioids besides fentanyl, the absolute number of synthetic opioid deaths occurring in a year such as 2014 should not be considered a proxy for the number of fentanyl deaths in a year. Second, law enforcement drug submissions might vary over time and geographically because of differences or changes in law enforcement testing practices and drug enforcement activity, which might underestimate or over-estimate the number of fentanyl submissions in certain states. Third, findings and implications are restricted to 27 states. Finally, testing for fentanyl deaths might vary across states because toxicologic testing protocols for drug over-doses vary across states and local jurisdictions.

The Secretary of Health and Human Services has launched an initiative to reduce opioid misuse, abuse, and overdose by expanding medication-assisted treatment, increasing the availability and use of naloxone, and promoting safer opioid prescribing *(10)*. Efforts should focus on 1) improving timeliness of opioid surveillance to facilitate faster identification and response to spikes in fentanyl overdoses; 2) expanding testing for fentanyl and fentanyl analogs by physicians, treatment programs, and medical examiners/coroners in high-burden states; 3) expanding evidence-based harm reduction and expanding naloxone access, with a focus on persons using heroin; 4) implementing programs that increase linkage and access to medication-assisted treatment, with a focus on persons using heroin; 5) increasing collaboration between public health and public safety; and 6) planning rapid response in high-burden states and states beginning to experience increases in fentanyl submissions or deaths.

ACKNOWLEDGEMENTS

Tamara Haegerich, PhD, Nina Shah, MS, Division of Unintentional Injury Prevention, National Center for Injury Prevention and Control, CDC.

1. How can consistent forms for reporting incidents help governments plan for public health and safety?

2. Is it the responsibility of doctors and police to plan how to deal with people who overdose on drugs?

"EU AIMS TO AVOID OPIOID EPIDEMIC," BY BART MORLION, FROM *HEALTHCARE IN EUROPE*, FEBRUARY 11, 2016

In the USA, there is already talk of an "opioid epidemic." Whereas in the past 20 years some 100,000 people died directly or indirectly through prescribed opioids, reports indicate that more than 16,000 died in 2010 alone. Since the sales of opioid analgesics quadrupled between 1999 and 2010 recent debates have intensified surrounding the use of opioids for non-tumour-related pain in the USA, as well as Canada and Australia, with dependency and risks moving into the spotlight. The US Food and Drug Administration (FDA) restricted the indication for prescribing opioids and demanded that manufacturers conduct more studies on risks, such as abuse, addiction, excessive pain sensitivity, overdoses and fatalities.

This trend has reached Europe: The European Council has initiated a discussion of abuse and dependency on medications, with a focus on opioid analgesics.

European pain experts are worried about this development. Professor Bart Morlion, president-elect of the European Pain Federation EFIC, warned those attending the 9th Congress of the European Pain Federation, in Vienna, against exaggerated caution; not to toss the baby out with the bathwater: "Opioids provide important therapeutic options in bringing relief from acute and chronic pain. We should not re-stigmatise these analgesics, but instead clarify how they can be used safely and effectively."

The professor is emphatically against generalizing USA data and applying them to Europe. The abuse problem is virulent mainly in North America and Australia, since prescriptions are less regulated than in Europe, where access is strictly regulated by special prescription forms, or the addictive substances registry: "Reports on increasing problems with opioids, particularly from North America, are mostly related to long-term prescription with a lack of careful patient selection and patient reassessment." In some US states, so-called "pill mills" – medical facilities that prescribe controlled substances without regard for guidelines and indicators – are allegedly responsible for numerous opioid-related fatalities. "There are certainly many good reasons for the increase in prescription rates. However, in future more care needs to be taken to ensure that opioids are the right choice for the individual patient," Prof. Morlion emphasizes. "Opioids are not without side effects. For this reason they should only be prescribed in cases where there is a good balance between pain relief and side effects, where there are long-term benefits, and where other methods of treatment have failed."

It cannot be that abuse in some parts of the world leads to a global call for restrictions that could mean insurmountable hurdles for those urgently needing opioids for pain control.

Therefore, the European professional society seeks a reasonable approach between dramatic undersupply, over-prescription and the abuse problem. EFIC commissioned a working group to prepare Europe-wide recommendations for an appropriate and responsible handling of opioids, especially in long-term therapy of chronic pain. With recommendations expected this autumn, Prof. Morlion expects the "... guidelines should provide doctors throughout Europe with support and advice for optimal use of opioid analgesics that's easy to put into practice."

PROFILE:

Anaesthesiologist, intensive care physician and pain expert Bart Morlion MD is president-elect of the European Pain Federation EFIC. He studied at the University of Leuven, Belgium, and completed a specialist residency at the Ruhr University, Bochum, Germany. He returned to Leuven in 1998 to become professor in the Department of Cardiovascular Sciences and head of the multidisciplinary pain centre. From 2006 until 2012 Morlion presided over the Belgian Pain Society and is the principal investigator in 28 national and international multi-centre clinical trials (Phases II, III and IV).

1. How is the use of opioids regulated differently in different countries?

2. How can these different regulations have different effects on the abuse of opioids?

CHAPTER 2

WHAT THE GOVERNMENT SAYS

Statistics published by the American government show that from the years 1999 to 2014, the drug poisoning death rate involving heroin increased from 0.7 to 3.4 deaths per 100,000 people, with most of that increase happening since 2011. The poisoning death rate involving opioid analgesics increased from 1.4 to 5.9 deaths per 100,000 residents. To put those numbers in some perspective, in 2014 the death rate for all kinds of drug poisoning was 14.7 per 100,000. During those same fifteen years, the number of people who caught pertussis (whooping cough), a disease that can be prevented by a vaccine, increased from 4.04 to 9.12 cases per 100,000 American people.[1]

For the United Nations Office on Drugs and Crime (UNDOC), the focus of their *World Drug Report 2016* was on long-term alternative development, aimed at developing alternative sources of income for farmers who depend on growing opium poppies for heroin or coca leaves for cocaine. The UNDOC notes that many factors keep these farmers dependent on growing these plants for the international drug trade; they don't benefit from most development programs, they have little or no security of land ownership, and their rural communities are often subject to social and political problems imposed on them. Cutting down on opium production from the start might be a good way for the government to deal with increasing rates of opioid addictions and opium-related deaths.

"MIND OVER MATTER: PRESCRIPTION PAIN MEDICATIONS (OPIOIDS)," BY THE NATIONAL INSTITUTE FOR DRUG ABUSE FOR TEACHERS, 2014

Maybe you've heard of drugs called heroin, morphine, or codeine. These are examples of opioids. If someone uses opioids again and again, his or her brain is likely to become dependent on them.

THE BRAIN'S RESPONSE TO OPIOIDS

Hi, my name's Sara Bellum. Welcome to my magazine series exploring the brain's response to drugs. In this issue, we'll investigate the fascinating facts about opioids.

If you've ever seen The Wizard of Oz, then you've seen the poppy plant—the source of a type of drug called an opioid. When Dorothy lies down in a field of poppies, she falls into a deep sleep. No wonder the Latin name of this plant—*Papaver somniferum*—means "the poppy that makes you sleepy." Opioids can be made from opium, which comes from the poppy plant, or they can be made in a lab. Either way, they can be helpful medicines—they are used as powerful painkillers, they are sometimes prescribed to control severe diarrhea, and they can also be found in cough medicine. Maybe you've heard of drugs called Vicodin, morphine, or codeine. These are examples of opioids. When used properly as medicine, they can be very helpful. But opioids used without a prescription, or taken in other ways or for different reasons than the doctor prescribed, can be dangerous and addictive.

Heroin is another example of an opioid, but it isn't used as a medicine—it's used to get high.

HOW DO OPIOIDS WORK?

Opioids look like chemicals in your brain and body that attach to tiny parts on nerve cells called opioid receptors. Scientists have found three types of opioid receptors: *mu, delta,* and *kappa* (named after letters in the Greek alphabet). Each of these receptors plays a different role. For example, *mu* receptors are responsible for opioids' pleasurable effects and their ability to relieve pain.

Opioids act on many places in the brain and nervous system, including:

- the **limbic system**, which controls emotions. Here, opioids can create feelings of pleasure, relaxation, and contentment.
- the **brainstem**, which controls things your body does automatically, like breathing. Here, opioids can slow breathing, stop coughing, and reduce feelings of pain.
- the **spinal cord**, which receives sensations from the body before sending them to the brain. Here too, opioids decrease feelings of pain, even after serious injuries.

Whether it is a medication like Vicodin or a street drug like heroin, the effects of opioids (and many other drugs) depend on how much you take and how you take them. If they are injected, they act faster and more intensely. If opioids are swallowed as pills, they take longer to reach the brain and are much safer.

HOW DOES SOMEONE BECOME ADDICTED TO OPIOIDS?

Long-term opioid use changes the way nerve cells work in the brain. This happens even to people who take opioids for a long time to treat pain, as prescribed by their doctor.

The nerve cells grow used to having opioids around, so that when they are taken away suddenly, the person can have lots of unpleasant feelings and reactions. These are known as withdrawal symptoms.

Have you ever had the flu? You probably had aching, fever, sweating, shaking, or chills. These are similar to withdrawal symptoms, but withdrawal symptoms are much worse.

That is why use of opioids should be carefully watched by a doctor—so that a person knows how much to take and when, as well as how to stop taking them to lessen the chances of withdrawal symptoms. Eventually, the cells will work normally again, but that takes time.

Someone who is addicted to opioids has other problems as well. For example, they keep taking the drug even though it may be having harmful effects on their life and their health. They have strong urges to take the drug—called cravings—and they no longer feel satisfied by natural rewards (like chocolate, TV, or a walk on the beach).

SURPRISING FACTS

Opioids can make you throw up—this can even happen to someone given opioids by a doctor—which is why many people don't like taking them.

Your brain makes its own versions of opioids, called endogenous opioids. These chemicals act just like opioid drugs, attaching to opioid receptors in your brain. Endogenous opioids help your body control pain. If you've ever felt pleasantly relaxed after exercising a lot, that feeling was probably caused by the release of these natural chemicals (sometimes called "endorphins") in your brain.

THE SEARCH CONTINUES

There is still a lot that scientists don't know about the effects of opioids on the brain. Maybe someday you will make the next big discovery!

Until then, join me—Sara Bellum—in the magazines in my series, as we explore how drugs affect the brain and nervous system.

1. In what ways can new resources on opioids be more useful than older ones?

"FACT SHEET: OBAMA ADMINISTRATION ANNOUNCES PUBLIC AND PRIVATE SECTOR EFFORTS TO ADDRESS PRESCRIPTION DRUG ABUSE AND HEROIN USE," BY THE WHITE HOUSE OFFICE OF THE PRESS SECRETARY, OCTOBER 25, 2015

Prescription drug abuse and heroin use have taken a heartbreaking toll on too many Americans and their families, while straining law enforcement and treatment programs. Today, the President will travel to West Virginia to hear directly from individuals and families affected by this epidemic and the health care professionals, law enforcement officers, and community leaders working to prevent addiction and respond to its aftermath.

As part of today's event, the President will announce federal, state, local and private sector efforts aimed at addressing the prescription drug abuse and heroin epidemic. These include commitments by more than 40 provider groups – representing doctors, dentists, advanced practice registered nurses, physician assistants, physical therapists and educators -- that more than 540,000 health care providers will complete opioid prescriber training in the next two years. In addition, CBS, ABC, the New York Times, Google, the National Basketball Association, Major League Baseball and other companies will donate millions of dollars in media space for PSAs about the risks of prescription drug misuse produced by the Partnership for Drug-Free Kids.

Today, the **President issued a Memorandum to Federal Departments and Agencies** directing two important steps to combat the prescription drug abuse and heroin epidemic:

- ***Prescriber Training***:   First, to help ensure that health care professionals who prescribe opioids are properly trained in opioid prescribing and to establish the Federal Government as a model, the Presidential Memorandum requires Federal Departments and Agencies to provide training on the prescribing of these medications to Federal health care professionals who prescribe controlled substances as part of their Federal responsibilities.

- ***Improving Access to Treatment***: Second, to improve access to treatment for prescription drug abuse and heroin use, the Presidential Memorandum directs Federal Departments and Agencies that directly provide, contract to provide, reimburse for, or otherwise facilitate access to health benefits, to conduct a review to identify barriers to medication-assisted treatment for opioid use disorders and develop action plans to address these barriers.

More Americans now die every year from drug overdoses than they do in motor vehicle crashes and the majority of those overdoses involve prescription medications. Health care providers wrote 259 million prescriptions for opioid pain medications in 2012 – enough for every American adult to have a bottle of pills. Opioids are a class of prescription pain medications that includes hydrocodone, oxycodone, morphine, and methadone. Heroin belongs to the same class of drugs, and four in five heroin users started out by misusing prescription opioid pain medications.

In 2010, the President released his first National Drug Control Strategy, which emphasized the need for action to address opioid use disorders and overdose, while ensuring that individuals with pain receive safe, effective treatment. Since then, the Administration has supported and expanded community-based efforts to prevent drug use, pursue 'smart on crime' approaches to drug enforcement, improve prescribing practices for pain medication, increase access to treatment, work to reduce overdose deaths, and support the millions of Americans in recovery.

The most recent data show that the rate of overdoses involving prescription pain medication is leveling off, although it remains at an unacceptably high level. But the dramatic rise in heroin-related overdoses – which nearly doubled between 2011 and 2013 – shows the opioid crisis is far from over.

STATE, LOCAL AND PRIVATE SECTOR ACTIONS ANNOUNCED TODAY INCLUDE:

- More than 40 provider groups – including physicians, dentists, advanced practice registered nurses, physician assistants, physical therapists and educators -- committed to:
- Have more than 540,000 health care providers complete opioid prescriber training in the next two years;
- Double the number of physicians certified to prescribe buprenorphine for opioid use disorder treatment, from 30,000 to 60,000 over the next three years;
- Double the number of providers that prescribe naloxone--a drug that can reverse an opioid overdose;
- Double the number of health care providers registered with their State Prescription Drug Monitoring Programs in the next two years; and
- Reach more than 4 million health care providers with awareness messaging on opioid abuse, appropriate prescribing practices, and actions providers can take to be a part of the solution in the next two years.

Groups include the American Medical Association, American Osteopathic Association, American Academy of Family Physicians, American College of Emergency Physicians, American Academy of Hospice and Palliative Medicine, American Congress of Obstetricians and Gynecologists, American Academy of Pediatricians, American Society of Anesthesiologists, American Society of Addiction Medicine, American College of Osteopathic Internists, American Pain Society, American Academy of Addiction Psychiatry, American College of Physicians, American College of Osteopathic Emergency

Physicians, American Academy of Pain Medicine, Interstate Postgraduate Medical Association, Physician's Institute, American College of Osteopathic Surgeons, American College of Osteopathic Family Physicians, American Osteopathic Academy of Addiction Medicine, American Medical Student Association, American Medical Women's Association, Michigan Osteopathic Association, Ohio Osteopathic Association, Massachusetts Medical Society, Washington Osteopathic Medical Association, New Mexico Medical Society, California Academy of Family Physicians, Conjoint Committee on Continuing Education, Collaboration for REMS Education, American Nurses Association, American Association of Nurse Practitioners, American Association of Nurse Anesthetists, Association of Women's Health, Obstetric and Neonatal Nurses, American Psychiatric Nurses Association, American Association of Colleges of Nursing, National Association of Clinical Nurse Specialists, Nurse Practitioner Healthcare Foundation, American Academy of Physician Assistants, Physician Assistant Education Association, American Dental Association, American Physical Therapy Association, Association of American Medical Colleges, American Public Health Association, and Medscape.

- **CVS Health** will allow CVS/pharmacy to dispense naloxone without patients needing to present an individual prescription pursuant to a standing order from a physician or collaborative practice agreement in an additional 20 states in 2016 and will launch a new drug abuse prevention program called Pharmacists Teach, where its pharmacists will make 2,500 presentations in high school health classes.

Rite Aid will train 6,000 pharmacists on naloxone use over the next 12 months, and expand their naloxone dispensing program to additional states. **The National Association of Chain Drug Stores** will continue to educate their 125 chain member companies (40,000 pharmacies with 175,000 pharmacists) about opioid overdose and naloxone. **The National Community Pharmacists Association**, representing 23,000 pharmacies with over 62,000 pharmacists, will be distributing inserts to community pharmacists that highlight safe drug disposal and naloxone. The **American Pharmacists Association**, with an outreach capability to more than 250,000 individuals, will educate pharmacists, student pharmacists, and stakeholders through a new Resource Center on opioid use, misuse, and abuse. The **American Society of Health-System Pharmacists** will provide training and resources to 40,000 pharmacists, student pharmacists and pharmacy technicians. The **National Association of Boards of Pharmacy** will enhance access to prescription drug monitoring program data to thousands more physicians and pharmacists in Arizona, Delaware, Kentucky, and North Dakota in 2016.

- The **Fraternal Order of Police** will provide their 330,000 members with an Opioid Overdose Resuscitation card to help identify and respond to overdoses. They will also educate thousands of their members through in-person and webinar overdose prevention trainings over the next year. The **International Association of Chiefs of Police** will host several educational sessions on the role of law enforcement in overdose revention at its annual conference and will also hold an overdose prevention training webinar for its members.

- The **National Association of Counties, National League of Cities**, and **United States Conference of Mayors**, in conjunction with **U.S. Communities Purchasing Alliance** and **Premier, Inc.**, will secure industry-leading discounts for tens of thousands of public agencies on naloxone and medications for treatment through their purchasing program that pools the purchasing power of state and local governments.
- To support the **Partnership for Drug-Free Kids'** media campaign over the next year to increase the education and awareness of young people and their parents about the risks of prescription drug misuse, **CBS Television Network, Turner Broadcasting, ABC owned and operated TV Stations, The New York Times, Google, Café Mom**, and **Meredith** are committing more than $20 million in donated airtime and advertising space, and additional commitments are expected. The **National Basketball Association** and **Major League Baseball** will also run public service announcements across their respective media assets. The Partnership is also releasing an online toolkit to help local governments, law enforcement, and other community jurisdictions implement local drug disposal programs.
- Because prescription opioid misuse is a growing concern in high school and college athletics, The **National Collegiate Athletic Association** will educate more than 30,000 student-athletes about the dangers of prescription drug misuse, publish best practices to support student-athlete behavioral health, and sponsor the third Step UP! Bystander Intervention conference to equip educators to assist their students and student-athletes in intervening with peers on a host of behavioral con-

cerns, including prescription drug misuse. The **National Association of High School Coaches** will launch a drug prevention awareness campaign that will be shared with 320,000 head high school coaches and approximately 60,000 high school administrators. The **American College of Sports Medicine** will mobilize more than 500,000 sports medicine professionals in support of their *"Better Move Campaign"* to reduce the overuse and overdose of prescription pain medications. **The National Athletic Trainers' Association** will share educational materials on opioid misuse prevention to 40,000 athletic trainers. The **National Interscholastic Athletic Administrators Association** will educate its membership of over 9,500 secondary school athletic administrators about substance use and its relationship to health and performance through its professional development program.

- The **National PTA**, which has more than four million members, will distribute prescription drug misuse awareness and educational materials to its members and promote them through its digital assets.

- Governors and local governments will be taking new actions to reduce opioid misuse and overdose throughout the next year. The **National Association of Counties** will mobilize more county leaders to implement smart strategies to reduce opioid misuse and overdose through their *Safe and Secure Counties Initiative*. The **National Governors Association** will launch a *Developing Effective State Responses to the Heroin Epidemic* project to help states identify and implement effective strategies for reducing heroin use and overdose. The **United States Conference of Mayors**, through its new Substance Abuse, Prevention, and Recovery

Services Task Force, will identify effective prevention, intervention, treatment, recovery, and support services to promote to city mayors nationwide.

- The **Harm Reduction Coalition** will increase the number of naloxone doses provided through its network of partners from 130,000 in 2013 to 400,000 in 2016 and will work with 10 state prisons to provide training and naloxone kits to 4,000 pre-release inmates and their family members in 2016. They will also convene a national summit on how syringe services programs are integrating broader prevention, counseling, care and treatment initiatives in response to the opioid epidemic.

- **The Elks National Drug Awareness Program** will purchase and install at least 500 prescription drug disposal boxes in communities where heroin use and prescription drug abuse are most prevalent by the end of 2016.

- The **Community Anti-Drug Coalitions of America** will train 2,000 youth leaders across the country about the dangers of prescription drug abuse; train 12,000 youth and adult leaders on effective prescription drug abuse prevention strategies; and hold 100 community forums to mobilize youth and adult leaders on this issue in 2016.

- **The Dr. Oz Show** will launch a campaign leading up to a *National Night of Conversation* event on November 19 to encourage parents to talk with their children about prescription pain medications, heroin, and other drugs. Dr. Oz will promote this prevention initiative to millions of Americans through his show, other media appearances, and his nationally syndicated newspaper column.

- The **Blue Cross Blue Shield Association** is launching a national opioid use awareness campaign to help communities find local solutions for prevention and treatment.

- **The American Physical Therapy Association** will reach more than 2.5 million members of the public and more than 100,000 of its members through awareness campaigns about the benefits of physical therapy as a potential alternative to prescription pain medications. The **National Association of Social Workers** will expand training for its 132,000 members on treatment of substance use disorders including opioid misuse, and will train school social workers to partner with parent and school organizations on prevention efforts. The **American Public Health Association** will provide continuing education credit training on prescription drug overdose to more than 1,500 health providers and distribute prescription drug misuse awareness materials to over 300,000 public health professionals.
- The **American Association of Colleges of Nursing**, the **Association of American Medical Colleges**, and the **Physician Assistant Education Association** will share professional guidance and best practices to better educate the next generation of health care workers on opioid misuse and substance use disorders.
- **WebMD** and **Medscape** are committed to increasing awareness of opioid issues and informing and educating consumer and professional audiences. In December, WebMD and Medscape will produce a report on consumer and health care professionals' awareness of issues surrounding opioid use. The report will be based on findings of a joint survey of consumers and health care professionals and explore issues ranging from prescribing practices and guidelines to the use and disposal of the drugs, as well as general levels of awareness around their misuse.

ADDITIONAL FEDERAL ACTIONS ANNOUNCED TODAY INCLUDE:

- The **Drug Enforcement Administration** announced that it will continue its National Prescription Drug Take-Back Day program events in the spring and fall of 2016. As the President highlighted in a recent Weekly Address, Take-Back Day aims to provide a safe, convenient, and responsible means of disposing of unused prescription drugs, while educating the public about the dangers of misusing medications.

- The **Department of Health and Human Services** (HHS) will undertake a review of how pain management is evaluated by patient satisfaction surveys used by hospitals and other health care providers, including review of how the questions these surveys use to assess pain management may relate to pain management practices and opioid prescribing.

- The **Centers for Disease Control and Prevention** (CDC) will invest $8.5 million on the development of tools and resources to help inform prescribers about appropriate opioid prescribing; track data on prescribing trends; research, develop, and evaluate clinical quality improvement measures and programs on opioid prescribing; and improve public understanding of the risks and benefits of opioid use.

- **HHS** also launched HHS.gov/opioids as a one-stop federal resource with tools and information for families, health care providers, law enforcement, and other stakeholders on prescription drug abuse and heroin use prevention, treatment, and response.

- **U.S. Surgeon General Vivek Murthy** is developing an education campaign for doctors, dentists and other health care professionals who prescribe opioid pain medications. Earlier this month, Dr. Murthy also announced that work has begun on the first-ever Surgeon General's Report on substance use, addiction and health scheduled for publication in 2016.
- **Centers for Medicare and Medicaid Services** (CMS) will release an Information Bulletin to States by the end of the year on steps States can take through their Medicaid preferred drug lists (PDLs) and other utilization management mechanisms to reduce the risk of overdose. This includes a recommendation that they consider removing methadone from their PDLs for pain management. The Centers for Disease Control and Prevention has found that the use of methadone in pain treatment is associated with a disproportionately high number of overdose deaths compared to other opioid pain relievers.
- This fall, **CMS** is testing three new Medicare prescription drug plan measures designed to identify potential opioid overutilization, with the goal of proposing publicly reportable measures for Part D drug plans next year. These measures are based on the work of the Pharmacy Quality Alliance.
- **The Department of Veterans Affairs** will lead a research initiative to evaluate non-opioid alternative approaches to pain management. The **Department of Defense** (DoD) and VA are developing a standardized pain management curriculum for widespread use in education and training programs.
- The **Bureau of Indian Affairs** (BIA) and the

Indian Health Service will provide BIA police officers and investigators the overdose reversal drug naloxone and training on its use. In 2016, the BIA, through the United States Indian Police Academy, will provide training to all BIA and tribal police officer cadets in recognizing opioid use disorders and overdose symptoms.

- The White House will host a **Champions of Change** event this spring to highlight individuals in communities across the country who are leading the fight to respond to prescription drug abuse and heroin use.

TODAY'S ACTIONS BUILD ON THE ADMINISTRATION'S COMMITMENT TO CONFRONTING THIS EPIDEMIC:

In 2010, the President released his first National Drug Control Strategy, emphasizing the need for action to address opioid use disorders and overdose, while ensuring that individuals with pain receive safe, effective treatment. The next year, the White House released its national Prescription Drug Abuse Prevention Plan to outline our goals for addressing prescription drug abuse and overdose.

The President's Fiscal Year 2016 budget includes $133 million in new investments aimed at addressing the opioid epidemic, including expanding state-level prescription drug overdose prevention strategies, medication-assisted treatment programs, and access to the overdose-reversal drug naloxone.

Examples of additional actions by the Administration to address the opioid epidemic include:

COMMUNITY PREVENTION AND OVERDOSE RESPONSE

- In 2015, the CDC launched the *Prescription Drug Overdose: Prevention for States Program*, which provided $20 million to states to support strategies to improve prescribing practices and prevent opioid overdose deaths.
- Through the National Take Back Days to remove unused prescription drugs from the community, the Drug Enforcement Administration (DEA) has collected more than 5.5 million pounds of medication and introduced several new ways to dispose of unused prescription drugs – including pre-paid return-mail packages. DEA also finalized a new rule making it easier for communities to establish ongoing drug take-back programs.
- In 2012, the Department of Veterans Affairs established an Opioid Safety Initiative to enhance safe and effective pain care for veterans. VA medical centers have filled more than 6,500 naloxone kit prescriptions, and VA's efforts to make opioid overdose kits available has resulted in at least 100 lives saved.
- With support from the Department of Justice (DOJ) and other funders, 49 states have established Prescription Drug Monitoring Programs to help prescribers identify potential opioid misuse issues.
- In 2015, HHS announced a targeted initiative to combat opioid related overdose, death, and dependence focused on increasing prescriber training, increasing the use of the overdose reversal drug

naloxone, and expanding the use of medication-assisted treatment.

- The federal government is expanding access to prescription drug monitoring program data throughout federal agencies. DoD's Pharmacy Data Transaction Service automatically screens all new medication orders against a patient's computerized medication history and permits DoD to monitor for concerning drug usage patterns. DoD's Polypharmacy Medication Analysis Reporting is being used to identify high risk active duty service members based on their medication use and emergency department encounters. The Indian Health Service has successfully piloted integrating this data into their electronic systems, and a pilot to integrate data into the workflow of physicians in the DoD health system is slated to launch in 2016.
- The DOJ Bureau of Justice Assistance released a Law Enforcement Naloxone Toolkit to support law enforcement agencies in establishing naloxone programs. The toolkit has been downloaded more than 2,200 times in the last year.
- DOD is ensuring that opioid overdose reversal kits and training are available to every first responder on military bases or other areas under its control.
- The Office of National Drug Control Policy supports local Drug Free Communities coalitions to reduce youth substance use through evidence-based prevention. In recent years, hundreds of these coalitions have specifically focused on prescription drug misuse issues in their areas.

TREATMENT

- Thanks to the Affordable Care Act, substance use disorder and mental health services are essential health benefits that are required to be covered by health plans in the Health Insurance Marketplace.
- New rules finalized by this Administration ensure that covered mental health and substance use disorder benefits are comparable to medical and surgical benefits.
- HHS is investing up to $100 million in Affordable Care Act funding to expand substance use disorder treatment, with a focus on medication-assisted treatment for opioid use disorders, in community health centers across the country.
- HHS Secretary Burwell announced that the Department will engage in rulemaking related to the prescribing of buprenorphine-containing products approved by the FDA for treatment of opioid dependence to expand access to medication-assisted treatment for opioid use disorders. HHS will take a strategic approach in order to minimize diversion and ensure evidence-based treatment.
- The CDC has been working over the last year with clinical experts and other stakeholders to develop new, peer-reviewed guidelines on prescribing opioids for chronic pain outside end of life settings to help improve the way opioids are prescribed and ensure patients have access to safer, more effective chronic pain treatment, while reducing opioid misuse and overdose.
- HHS recently awarded $11 million in new grants to States to support medication-assisted treatment and

$1.8 million to help rural communities purchase naloxone and train first responders in its use.

ENFORCEMENT AND SUPPLY REDUCTION

- The White House Office of National Drug Control Policy's High Intensity Drug Trafficking Areas program is funding an unprecedented network of public health and law enforcement partnerships to address the heroin threat across 15 states.
- In October of 2015, DOJ's Office of Community Oriented Policing Services (COPS Office) awarded $6 million through the Anti-Heroin Task Force Program, which is designed to advance public safety by providing funds to investigate illicit activities related to the distribution of heroin or unlawful distribution of prescriptive opioids, or unlawful heroin and prescription opioid traffickers through statewide collaboration.
- DOJ's enforcement efforts include targeting the illegal opioid supply chain, thwarting doctor-shopping attempts, and disrupting so-called "pill mills."
- DOJ has cracked down on those who use the Internet to buy and sell controlled substances.
- DEA agents and investigators are integrating with other federal, state, and local law enforcement officers in 66 Tactical Diversion Squads stationed across 41 states, Puerto Rico, and the District of Columbia. Outcomes of this effort include the largest pharmaceutical-related takedown in the DEA's history in an operation that resulted in 280 arrests.
- Since 2007, through the Merida Initiative, the Department of State has been working with the Government of

Mexico to help build the capacity of Mexico's law enforcement and justice sector institutions to disrupt drug trafficking organizations and to stop the flow of illicit drugs including heroin from Mexico to the United States.

1. What do you think would be the most effective plan of action against opioid abuse listed here?

2. What do you think would be the least? Why?

"FENTANYL CRACKDOWN COULD BRING DEADLIER DRUGS, EXPERT SAYS: HEALTH CANADA RESTRICTS IMPORTS OF MATERIALS FOR DRUG LINKED TO OVERDOSE EPIDEMIC," BY JEREMY J. NUTTALL, FROM *THE TYEE*, SEPTEMBER 1, 2016

Drug policy experts worry that the federal government's efforts to limit access to chemicals used to make the deadly drug fentanyl will result in even more dangerous drugs on the streets.

Health Canada announced plans for the new restrictions Wednesday, citing RCMP reports of increased domestic production of fentanyl for the illegal drug market. A recent study by Vancouver Coastal Health found 86 per cent of the drugs tested at Insite, the city's safe injection site, contain the opioid. The federal department hopes to reduce that by restricting access to six chemicals used to make fentanyl under the Controlled Drugs and Substances Act.

But Donald MacPherson, director of the Canadian Drug Policy Coalition, said making the chemicals used to make fentanyl harder to get could just lead to production of even more dangerous drugs. "We're caught in a vicious circle of having to further restrict dangerous things," MacPherson said. "I just don't think that drug prohibition in that sense has worked."

History shows more dangerous drugs arrive with each crackdown, he said, pointing out that fentanyl wasn't popular until Oxycontin was made harder to get.

MacPherson said people need access to safer drugs. Instead, he added, the restrictions could lead to more dangerous drugs once fentanyl becomes harder to produce.

Coquitlam-Port Coquitlam Member of Parliament Ron McKinnon said he understands the concerns, but the fentanyl crisis needs to be addressed. "If we can control the materials they use to make this stuff better, hopefully we can stem the tide of death that's happening out here and across the country," McKinnon said.

The fentanyl crisis has become "critical," the Liberal MP said, citing the overdose death of 16-year-old Gwynevere Staddon in a Starbucks washroom in suburban Port Moody earlier this month.

Health Canada's announcement mentioned McKinnon's private member's bill, the Good Samaritan Drug Overdose Act, as another tool in the fight against overdose deaths. The bill, which the government supports, will give people amnesty from drug possession charges if they call 911 when someone has overdosed on drugs.

Last year 465 people in B.C. died of drug overdoses. By the end of July this year there had already been 433 deaths.

McKinnon said the new restrictions will make it harder to buy the materials used to make fentanyl and easier for authorities to track purchasers, giving them more power to make a "serious dent" in the networks trafficking the drug. "People get into this drug and they don't know they're getting into it and it's powerful, certainly more powerful than they're obviously expecting," he said. "We need to be able to stop the production and manufacturing of this drug if we can."

MacPherson said the government could reduce overdose deaths by repealing the Respect for Communities Act passed by the Conservatives last June. The legislation makes it harder to open safe injection sites in Canada by imposing more stringent requirements.

McKinnon said safe injection sites are an important part of fighting overdoses and agreed "another hard look" at the Respect for Communities Act is worthwhile.

The newly restricted chemicals are propionyl chloride, phenethyl-4-piperidone and its salts, 4-piperidone and its salts, norfentanyl and its salts, 1-phenethylpiperidin-4-ylide-nephenylamine and its salts and N-Phenyl-4-piperidinamine and its salts.

1. How can laws intended to reduce the illegal use of opioids be part of the problem instead of a solution?
2. In what ways can laws that allow a safe injection site actually reduce the dangerous use of opioids?

"OFFICIALS TRY TO STOP FAKE PRESCRIPTIONS, BUT ADDICTS REMAIN PERSISTENT," BY GABRIEL SANDLER, FROM *CRONKITE NEWS*, JANUARY 5, 2017

PHOENIX – In an unrelenting quest for painkillers, Arizona pill seekers embark on almost daily missions to obtain fake or stolen prescriptions and shop their pain among doctors. Sometimes, pharmacists report, patients try to get "multiple, multiple narcotic" prescriptions from "multiple, multiple doctors."

Though the Arizona State Board of Pharmacy and lawmakers have built ways to thwart prescription drug fraud, Arizona's addicts and abusers are equally persistent. A Cronkite News review of almost 800 "fraud alerts," which are regularly sent to the board by concerned medical professionals and pharmacists, details the extent to which doctors and pharmacists are confronted with people willing to try almost anything to get painkillers.

According to one alert, a woman received 130 narcotic prescriptions from 93 prescribers, dispensed by 41 pharmacies. Another patient "has had 50 visits over the past 12 months where a controlled substance prescription was filled. She has seen 22 different physicians/providers, and filled at 16 different pharmacies."

A Mesa pharmacist also reported a female patient bringing in a prescription for Promethazine with codeine in October, but after calling the woman's doctor, it was determined that the "prescription was written on either a stolen prescription pad or was created by the suspect."

Another alert, submitted by a dentist, describes a woman, brown hair, 5 feet 4 inches tall, claiming she needed Percocet because of a codeine allergy. According to the dentist, "patient appeared inebriated, incoherent at times, details of events changed with each telling. Came with a gentleman using a walker, both insistent that she be given Percocet, angry that I wouldn't provide it, left without paying."

Cronkite News conducted a four-month investigation into the rise of prescription opioid abuse in Arizona. In 2015, more than 2 million grams of oxycodone alone came into the state, the third-highest total per capita in the country.

Dozens of journalists at Arizona State University examined thousands of records and traveled across the state to interview addicts, law enforcement, public officials and health care experts. The goal: uncover the root of the epidemic, explain the ramifications and provide solutions.

Since 2010, more than 3,600 people have overdosed and died from opioids in Arizona. In 2015, the dead numbered 701 – the highest of any year before, or nearly two per day, according to an analysis by the Arizona Department of Health Services.

The state launched the fraud alert system in 2013. Although the alerts often contains the name, address, physical description and sometimes the Social Security number of the potential drug seeker, no one – not the police, not the pharmacy board, not anyone – is responsible for further investigation.

"(Following up) is not part of our statutes, or our responsibility," said the pharmacy board's Executive Director Kam Gandhi. "We're actually a conduit, we send off the information from what's provided to us. We're not the enforcer, (nor) generally follow up on it."

Rob Dobrowski, the board's information technologist, said the fraud alert system is just one way to provide "a public service to keep everyone informed on the ongoing fraudulent prescription activity."

The board also runs the Controlled Substances Prescription Monitoring Program, or CSPMP, which is supposed to keep doctors and pharmacists accountable for the drugs they prescribe and keep addicts from getting them. When a patient comes into a pharmacy with a prescription, pharmacists log the drugs into the CSPMP. Doctors who use the system then can see what medications a patient already has received.

The CSPMP launched in 2009, but doctors were not legally required to look at a patient's prescription history until the Legislature passed a mandate this year.

The physician groups took the position that (the mandate) "was not necessary, that it was overly burdensome, it would expose doctors to liability, it would take up their valuable time," Arizona State Sen. John Kavanagh said.

After 20 years of police work in New York City during the crack epidemic, along with ambulance experience and friends lost to overdoses, Kavanagh understands the perils of addiction. He sponsored the mandate to protect pharmacists, doctors and addicts alike. By looking at a year of a patient's prescription history, doctors can determine whether or not someone is in legitimate need of painkillers.

"One of the greatest harms is for a doctor to be inadvertently placed in the role of drug supplier," Kavanagh said. "(The mandate) was an attempt to prevent patients from gaming the system by going to multiple doctors."

The mandate was initially supposed to go into effect in January 2017, but has been pushed back to October 2017, eight years after the state established the program.

"It's something the doctors really need to be working on," said Teresa Stickler, owner and pharmacist at Melrose Pharmacy in Phoenix. "I know they're not going to do anything until they're forced to."

According to Gandhi CSPMP is still in its "infancy stage" in Arizona. "Being mandated is the first step in assisting with the (opioid) problem nationwide. ... The CSPMP prior to last year or even the year before that was very underutilized," he said.

Although it contains Arizona's up-to-date, real-time prescription drug data, CSPMP Director Elizabeth Dodge said her team's main role with the database, "is just maintaining the data and storing it (for medical professionals). It's not actually analyzing."

Every month, however, the CSPMP does generate a report that flags patients who have seen four or more doctors and four or more pharmacies, at which point Dodge's team will notify the patients' physicians. Her office also assists law enforcement with open investigations involving prescription drug use.

Before coming to Arizona, Dodge was a pharmacist in a retail setting for 14 years in Nevada, where she used their prescription monitoring program.

One of Dodge's main objectives is to make CSPMP profiles part of standard electronic health records among all health care providers. That way, a patient's prescription history would appear with the medical history.

The Centers for Disease Control and Prevention data reflects a number of state successes for monitoring programs. New York and Tennessee passed mandates for their prescription drug monitoring programs, and saw a 75 percent and 36 percent decline in doctor shopping, respectively.

In Florida, regulating pain clinics in combination with a monitoring program, which they called E-FORCSE, resulted in a 50 percent decrease in overdose deaths caused by oxycodone, the CDC reports.

In addition to 163 million controlled substance prescription records, Florida law enforcement in 2015 "requested and received more than 6,509 investigative reports from E-FORCSE staff to assist in active criminal investigations," according to Florida Surgeon General John Armstrong's testimonial in the most recent annual report.

In the report, there's optimism that with all states enacting monitoring programs, besides Missouri, they will "serve as an integral part of patient and public safety solutions addressing the national prescription drug epidemic."

Even though she'd like to see its website streamlined, Stickler, the Phoenix pharmacist, appreciates the CSPMP and believes it has helped her practice.

"I think it's great," Stickler said. "It's a great addition. I remember a pharmacy before the PMP came out, and you definitely had more abuse going on back then. Now that people can check on it, it's harder to abuse."

The CDC calls prescription drug monitoring, "the most promising state-level interventions to improve opioid prescribing, inform clinical practice, and protect patients at risk."

Arizona's CSPMP and fraud alert system are two ways the board is attempting to stymie the opioid epidemic.

The fraud alerts are available to anyone who signs up to receive them through the pharmacy board.

Although there is no follow up, it allows medical professionals to identify suspected pill seekers through the personal information they provide.

Stickler said there should be more education and public awareness about the fraud alert system. Still, she said she is reluctant to use the system because the information is made public.

"We have had three fake prescriptions for promethazine with codeine in the past two months. I would like to get that information to other pharmacies, but I would not like it to get into the hands of somebody else," Stickler explained. "People will know what we look for, and I don't think that's a good thing."

Since it launched, more than 800 fraud alert submissions have been sent.

Though Dodge said the main role of the CSPMP is to store the information provided by pharmacists, she encourages doctors to use it even before the mandate goes into effect.

The legislation behind the CSPMP is intended to, "improve the state's ability to identify controlled substance abusers or misusers and refer them for treatment, and to identify and stop diversion of prescription controlled substance drugs," according to the CSPMP website.

"The PMP is just a tool in a whole big spectrum of things," Dodge said. "But it is a really good tool, and my goal is to protect it and also at the same time make it really easy for people to use."

Kavanagh said the pharmacy board has approached him about getting codeine cough syrups added in the CSPMP, even if they do not always require a prescription.

The pharmacies are OK with this step, Kavanagh said, because "they don't want to be involved in fueling more opium illegally into the streets."

1. According to the article, "The CDC calls prescription drug monitoring, 'the most promising state-level interventions to improve opioid prescribing, inform clinical practice, and protect patients at risk.'" Do you agree or disagree? Why might these state programs ultimately fail?

2. Whose responsibility is it to implement drug monitoring? Should it be doctors, pharmacists, local governments, or a combination of all three?

CHAPTER 3

WHAT THE COURTS SAY

Existing laws for criminal drug offenses may need to be revised because of recent changes in the kinds of opioids being abused. Most of the current laws were passed before the invention of prescription opioids such as fentanyl or carfentanil, which are one hundred times stronger than morphine and among the most powerful opioids available. A single illegal dose of fentanyl or carfentanil can be unexpectedly potent and cause a fatal overdose. Yet, for one particular drug trafficking case in 2016, a Canadian judge declined to consider fentanyl as an aggravating factor. In that judge's opinion, it is the role of lawmakers to state clearly whether convictions involving fentanyl deserve a higher sentence than when lower-risk opioids or drugs are involved. Thus, the law in terms of fentanyl abuse, in particular, has not been completely clear.

"If the risk of death isn't deterring you from using drugs, the risk of going to jail for some period of time surely isn't going to do it," as criminal lawyer Mike Mulligan has said. "All of our efforts for many years to try to deal with drug use and drug addiction as a criminal justice matter have been utterly unsuccessful."[1] This is the difficulty of prosecuting and preventing the further criminal actions of those who are addicted to opioids.

EXCERPT FROM *STATE OF WISCONSIN V. ANDY J. PARISI*, FROM THE SUPREME COURT OF WISCONSIN, FEBRUARY 24, 2016

REVIEW of a decision of the Court of Appeals. *Affirmed.*

¶ 1 This is a review of an unpublished decision of the court of appeals, State v. Parisi, No. 2014AP1267–CR, unpublished slip op., 2015 WL 247894 (Wis. Ct.App. Jan. 21, 2015) (per curiam), which affirmed the Winnebago County circuit court's[1] judgment of conviction and denial of defendant Andy J. Parisi's ("Parisi") motion to suppress evidence of heroin possession.

¶ 2 The circuit court below upheld a warrantless draw of Parisi's blood as justified under the exigent circumstances exception to the warrant requirement of the Fourth Amendment to the United States Constitution and Article I, § 11 of the Wisconsin Constitution. The court of appeals below affirmed on different grounds. Relying on our decisions in State v. Foster, 2014, and State v. Kennedy, 2014, the court of appeals determined that the good faith exception to the exclusionary rule applied to prevent suppression of the drug-related evidence in this case.

¶ 3 We conclude that the blood draw in this case was constitutional because it was supported by exigent circumstances. We therefore need not address whether the good faith exception to the exclusionary rule also applies in this case. See State v. Tullberg,

2014 (declining to address State's argument that the good faith exception to the exclusionary rule justified warrantless blood draw where blood draw had been found constitutional under exigent circumstances doctrine).

I. FACTUAL BACKGROUND

¶ 4 On October 16, 2012, at 12:38 a.m., several officers were dispatched to an address in Winnebago County, Wisconsin, to respond to a report of a male subject who was possibly not breathing.[2] One of the officers who responded to the call was Officer Kaosinu Moua ("Officer Moua") of the Oshkosh Police Department, who arrived at the residence "within five to ten minutes or so" after dispatch along with "a couple other officers."

¶ 5 Officer Moua testified that when he arrived at the residence, "one of the roommates[,] I believe one of the girls was outside waving us—trying to get us directed to the proper residence." Officer Moua entered the residence. During the medical call, police officers, members of the Oshkosh Fire Department, and the four roommates who lived at the residence in question were at the residence.

¶ 6 Inside, a male individual was lying in the living room on the floor on his side. There was vomit on the floor and on the sofa. The individual was not immediately identified by Officer Moua because the individual "wasn't able to talk to" Moua or the other officers. Eventually, the individual was identified as Parisi.

¶ 7 Members of the fire department were "checking for [Parisi's] vitals and making sure he was breathing." Officer Benjamin Fenhouse ("Officer Fenhouse"), who arrived at the residence at an unspecified time, was told that Narcan had been administered to Parisi. Officer Fenhouse testified that he had seen Narcan administered "between five and ten times" in the course of his employment, and that Narcan is "usually administered for people who have over-dosed on heroin[,] and it reverses the effects and usually brings them back to a responsive state pretty rapidly."[3] According to Officer Fenhouse, the Narcan "work[ed]" when administered to Parisi.

¶ 8 Officer Moua spoke with two of the roommates, who said that they did not know why Parisi was ill because they had been asleep. The roommates explained that Parisi had come over between 9:00 p.m. and 9:30 p.m. to watch "the game." "After the game," Parisi told his friends "that he wanted to go to the gas station, get something to eat and drink, so he did walk to the gas station and walked back," alone. After midnight, and after the roommates had gone to sleep, one of the roommates went to get a drink of water and "could hear some[body] breathing hard or [somebody] having problems breathing." The room-mate entered the living room and saw Parisi.

¶ 9 There were a total of five to seven officers "working on [the] case" that evening.[4] Because at least one of the officers had had "prior contact involving drugs with" Parisi, there was "suspicion" that drug use had been the cause of Parisi's condition.

¶ 10 A search of the upstairs was performed. The officers located, in a room separate from the room in which Parisi was found, "a bindle of what looked to be heroin wrapped in tinfoil, some cut ends, and [a] marijuana pipe." Officer Moua testified that Parisi did not live at the residence, but that Officer Moua had been told by the roommates that "everybody had access to [the] room [where the drug-related items were found]."

¶ 11 Officer Moua testified that the officers were at the apartment investigating "probably about an hour."[5] At some point during the investigation, Parisi was taken to the hospital by ambulance. Some officers continued their investigation at the residence after Parisi's departure. Officer Fenhouse followed the ambulance to the hospital in order to "investigate a heroin overdose and obtain ... an evidentiary test of [Parisi's] blood." Officer Fenhouse estimated that he was at the residence "like 20 minutes to a half hour" before leaving with the ambulance. Officer Moua also followed the ambulance.

¶ 12 At the hospital, according to Officer Fenhouse, "Parisi's medical condition was[,] I guess for lack of a better term[,] up in the air. [Hospital staff] were tending to him and then it seemed things were getting better and then it would deteriorate again." At some point in time, Officer Fenhouse asked for

Parisi's consent to take a blood sample, but "did not get [it]." Officer Fenhouse asked a phlebotomist to draw a sample of Parisi's blood without Parisi's consent in order "[t]o analyze it for evidence of a crime … [specifically, for] evidence of heroin." When asked on direct examination whether "there [was] something beyond administration of Narcan that suggested" to Officer Fenhouse that Parisi might have used heroin, Officer Fenhouse responded:

I was on the scene for a period of time and then I went to [the hospital]. I was in contact with persons that were still on scene, mainly officers, who provided me information that there was evidence of drug use and that led the investigation in a way that it could be heroin overdose.

¶ 13 Officer Fenhouse filled out a form specifying, among other things, the time that Parisi's blood was drawn. The form originally read that Parisi's blood was taken at "1:55 a.m.," but that time was crossed out and the time "3:10" was written in its place. Next to "3:10" were initials belonging, apparently, to Officer Fenhouse and the phlebotomist. Officer Fenhouse testified that according to his report, the time on the form was changed because

[Parisi's] health deteriorated or there was something else happening inside the room where it didn't kind of go as planned. That was filled out and we were intending on drawing [Parisi's blood] at a certain time, however, based on the medical needs of Mr. Parisi, it was obtained at a later time.

¶ 14 Officer Fenhouse testified that in his experience—which consisted of the acquisition of "about 12" search warrants—it takes approximately two hours to obtain a search warrant. Officer Fenhouse did not attempt to obtain a search warrant prior to the blood draw. Later testing of Parisi's blood at the State Crime Lab "indicated the presence of opiates and morphine (a metabolite of heroin)."[6]

II. PROCEDURAL BACKGROUND

¶ 15 On March 25, 2013, the State filed a criminal complaint against Parisi, charging him with possession of narcotic drugs (heroin), second and subsequent offense, contrary to Wis. Stat. §§ 961.41(3g)(am), 939.50(3)(i), and 961.48(1)(b) (2013–14).[7] On June 14, 2013, Parisi filed a motion to suppress the evidence of drug possession taken from the draw of Parisi's blood as unconstitutionally obtained without a warrant and without consent.

¶ 16 On July 12, 2013, a hearing on Parisi's suppression motion was held in Winnebago County circuit court. The State argued that exigent circumstances justified the blood draw at issue because the rapid rate of heroin dissipation in the human body rendered obtaining a warrant infeasible. The State based its assertions in part on a scientific article that summarized various studies on the metabolism of heroin in the human body. See Elisabeth J. Rook et al., Pharmacokinetics and Pharmacokinetic Variability of Heroin and its Metabolites: Review of the Literature, 1 Current Clinical Pharmacology 109 (2006) ("Rook article"). The article was admitted without objection from the defense.[8]

¶ 17 The article defines heroin as "a semi-synthetic morphine derivative." Id. at 109. Before the circuit court, the State cited the article to explain that heroin breaks down in human blood into 6–monoacetylmorphine, which breaks down further into morphine. The State offered the relevant timeframes for the metabolism of heroin, as set forth in the Rook article: "When heroin is used, the heroin that's actually in the blood lasts just basically a few minutes, and I don't recall the exact numbers ... but it's in the neighborhood of five minutes.[9] ... 6–monoacteylmorphine was detected in plasma for one to three hours." The State did not dispute that morphine was detectable in the blood for some time thereafter, but argued that unlike 6–monoacetylmorphine, morphine "can be created by a number of different substances. It could indicate somebody used heroin and it's been a number of hours or it could indicate something like they used morphine and there are other prescription drugs that break down into morphine as well."

¶ 18 Thus, "while the presence of morphine in someone's blood is relevant to whether they possessed heroin, it's certainly not conclusive evidence." The thrust of the State's argument, then, was that

if it's going to be more than that one to three-hour range that means that the State would be losing what could be necessary evidence in proving possession of heroin. And in this case ... we don't know the exact time of use.... And it was approximately two and a half hours after the dispatch when the blood draw actually occurred.

The State concluded by arguing for a per se rule, maintaining that "in basically any case where we have heroin use, it's creating an exigency because of the short timeframe."

¶ 19 Parisi did not contest any of the scientific data set forth by the State. Nor did he contest Officer Fenhouse's testimony that obtaining a warrant required approximately two hours. Instead, he argued that a totality-of-the-circumstances analysis applied under Missouri v. McNeely (2013), and that, under the totality of the circumstances, no exigent circumstances justified the warrantless blood draw. In particular, Parisi argued: there was no evidence the officers knew the scientific evidence the State presented; evidence of heroin's metabolites in the blood could be coupled with corroborating evidence to show possession of heroin; there were multiple officers involved with the case, so at least one of them could have attempted to obtain a search warrant; and a search warrant could have been obtained while Parisi was in the process of being medically stabilized.

¶ 20 The circuit court denied Parisi's motion, finding that the warrantless blood draw was constitutional because it was supported by exigent circumstances. With regard to the elimination of heroin from the human body, the court stated:

The study that [the State] has included … does indicate generally that heroin does dissipate fairly quickly from the human body. I think it's safe to say that it dissipates quicker than that of alcohol and that the half-lives are such that the breakdown causes a fairly quick inability to detect the heroin in the blood.

However, the court refused to adopt a per se rule that the dissipation of heroin in the blood constitutes an exigent circumstance in all cases. The court instead used a totality-of-the-circumstances analysis, relying on Missouri v. McNeely. The court concluded:

In this case, it does appear that there [were] exigent circumstances that were present here in regards to the unknown time of intake of the substance, the delay that took place in trying to determine what the defendant may or may not have taken, and what his medical condition was, the delays that were involved in regards to the treatment of him at the hospital setting, the time that it would take for obtaining the warrant, the dissipation of the heroin within the human body, and the speed in which it does that[;] so I think those are all factors in this particular case. And when the [c]ourt does look at the totality of those factors, I do think that the officer was justified in not pursuing a warrant in this case.

¶ 21 On September 13, 2013, Parisi pled no contest to possession of narcotic drugs; the State agreed to dismissal of the second and subsequent offense enhancer. On November 25, 2013, the court withheld sentence and placed Parisi on probation for 24 months. On May 23, 2014, Parisi filed a notice of appeal.

¶ 22 On January 21, 2015, the court of appeals affirmed the circuit court's judgment of conviction and denial of Parisi's suppression motion in an unpublished decision. *See State v. Parisi*, (2015) (per curiam). The court of appeals upheld the search as constitutional under the good faith exception to the exclusionary rule. Id. ¶ 12.

¶ 23 The court of appeals explained that on the date that Officer Fenhouse ordered the blood drawn from Parisi, State v. Bohling, (1993), abrogated by Missouri v. McNeely, (2013), "was the law of this state." Parisi, unpublished slip op., ¶ 9. Bohling, the court of appeals reasoned, "held that the dissipation of alcohol in a person's bloodstream, alone, constituted an exigent circumstance justifying a warrantless blood draw." Id. Although Bohling was later abrogated by McNeely, the court of appeals cited two of our recent cases for the proposition that "the good faith exception precludes application of the exclusionary rule where police searched a suspect's blood without a warrant in objectively reasonable reliance on Bohling." Id., ¶11 (citing State v. Kennedy, 2014; State v. Foster, 2014).

¶ 24 Finding "no legal difference between drawing blood to test it for alcohol or controlled drugs," the court of appeals concluded that the challenged evidence in Parisi's case was "obtained in conformity with [Bohling]" and that Kennedy and Foster were "controlling precedent applicable to this case." *Id.*, ¶¶ 11–12. "Thus, regardless of whether the warrant-less blood draw of Parisi may or may not have been retroactively unlawful under new United States Supreme Court precedent, the good faith exception precludes application of the exclusionary rule to exclude the evidence obtained." Id., ¶12

¶ 25 On February 19, 2015, Parisi filed a petition for review in this court. On June 12, 2015, we granted the petition.

[...]

V. CONCLUSION

¶ 60 We conclude that the blood draw in this case was constitutional because it was supported by exigent circumstances. We therefore need not address whether the good faith exception to the exclusionary rule also applies in this case. See State v. Tullberg, 2014 (declining to address State's argument that the good faith exception to the exclusionary rule justified warrantless blood draw where blood draw had been found constitutional under exigent circumstances doctrine).

By the Court.—The decision of the court of appeals is affirmed.

¶ 61 ANN WALSH BRADLEY, J. (dissenting). The primary issue addressed by the majority is whether Parisi's warrantless blood draw is an exigent circumstance justifying an exception to the warrant requirement. If it is not, then the warrantless blood draw was a violation of the Fourth Amendment of the United States Constitution and the evidence obtained must be suppressed.

¶ 62 All agree that absent an emergency, search warrants are required for intrusions into the human body. Missouri v. McNeely, (2013) (citing Schmerber v. California, (1966)).

¶ 63 Likewise, it is undisputed that pursuant to McNeely a per se rule authorizing warrantless blood draws based on dissipation of evidence in the bloodstream is prohibited under the Fourth Amendment. See id. Nevertheless, the majority creates a per se rule by inventing a new best evidence rule for every heroin case, concluding that exigent circumstances exist due to the rapid speed at which heroin dissipates in the blood.

¶ 64 Not only does the majority opinion disregard McNeely's prohibition of a per se rule based on dissipation, it also ignores the circumstances under which McNeely directs that the police must always obtain a warrant. McNeely instructs that "where police officers can reasonably obtain a warrant before a blood sample can be drawn without significantly undermining the efficacy of the search, the Fourth Amendment mandates that they do so." Id. at 1561.

¶ 65 Contrary to the majority, I conclude that the State has failed to show there were exigent circumstances justifying an exception to the warrant requirement. During the approximately two and one-half hours available, at least one of the five to seven officers involved in the investigation could have and should have obtained a warrant. The warrantless blood draw violated Parisi's Fourth Amendment rights and the evidence resulting from it should be suppressed.[1] Therefore, I respectfully dissent.

I.

¶ 66 The majority determines that the circuit court's finding of exigent circumstances based on "the dissipation of ... heroin within the human body, and the speed in which it does that" were not clearly erroneous. Majority op. ¶ 38. According to the majority, "critical evidence of heroin use in Parisi's body was disappearing by the minute, and had been since an unknown time that evening." Majority op. ¶ 41.

¶ 67 Repeatedly, the majority focuses on dissipation. See, e.g., majority op. ¶ 45 ("a two-hour delay would risk the destruction of evidence in this case because of, among other things, the rapid dissipation of heroin in the blood"); see also majority op. ¶ 48 ("waiting two hours to obtain a warrant would 'significantly undermin[e] the efficacy' of a blood draw by leading to ambiguous test results; evidence of heroin or morphine use, rather than heroin use alone, might result if sufficient time has passed"); majority op. ¶ 50 ("the fact that morphine remains in the body for several hours after the ingestion of heroin does not mean that it would be unreasonable for Officer Fenhouse to believe that taking the time to obtain a search warrant in this case risked destruction of evidence of heroin use").

¶ 68 In asserting that the rapid dissipation of heroin is an exigent circumstance, the majority relies on scientific literature provided by the State. See Elisabeth J. Rook et al., Pharmacokinetics and the Pharmacokinetic Variability of Heroin and its Metabolites: Review of the Literature, 1 Current Clinical Pharmacology 109, 111 (2006). Of particular import is the scientific evidence that "[h]eroin converts to its first metabolite, 6–[mono]acetylmorphine[,] within a few minutes. 6–[mono]acetylmorphine then converts to morphine. 6–[mono]acetylmorphine is detectable in plasma for 1–3 hours after heroin use." Majority op. ¶ 43. According to the majority, heroin or its first metabolite, 6–monoacetylmorphine, are the most probative evidence of heroin use and therefore the best evidence. Majority op. ¶ 46.

¶ 69 The majority concedes that morphine is evidence of heroin use that remains in the blood for hours after heroin and 6–monoacetylmorphine dissipate. See, e.g., majority op. ¶ 50. Nevertheless, it rejects this evidence as not being sufficiently probative.[2] Consequently, the majority creates a best evidence rule in heroin cases.

¶ 70 Oddly, the majority ends up arguing that the very evidence of morphine the State wishes to preserve in the suppression motion is really not good enough because it is less probative than heroin or 6–

monoacetylmorphine. Majority op. ¶ 46. It contends, "Parisi might have a plausible defense to a charge based on heroin found in the residence and morphine found in his blood, but no defense to a charge based on heroin found in the residence and heroin or 6–monoacetylmorphine found in his blood." Majority op. ¶ 46.

II.

¶ 71 In our prior decisions, this court properly recognized that <u>McNeely</u> "changed the landscape of warrantless blood draws in Wisconsin." <u>State v. Tullberg</u>, 2014 <u>see also State v. Kennedy</u>, 2014, ("in 2013, the United States Supreme Court issued its decision in <u>McNeely</u>, effectively abrogating our holding in <u>Bohling</u> that the rapid dissipation of alcohol alone constitutes an exigent circumstance sufficient for law enforcement officers to order a warrantless investigatory blood draw.")[3] In <u>Kennedy</u>, this court concluded that under <u>McNeely</u>, "the Fourth Amendment does not allow such per se rules in the context of warrantless investigatory blood draws."

¶ 72 Despite this court's prior adherence to *McNeely*, the cornerstone of the majority's opinion rests on its repeated assertion that the rapid dissipation of heroin in the blood risks the destruction of evidence. *See, e.g.*, majority op. ¶¶ 40–45. Yet, the majority admonishes that this case "does not establish a per se rule that the dissipation of heroin in the blood always constitutes an exigency justifying a warrantless blood draw." Majority Op. ¶ 42.

¶ 73 Contrary to the above admonition, the author of the majority opinion got it right at oral argument. The State's argument, which the majority now adopts, is really "Bohling for heroin";

Justice Ziegler: OK, but it has never been the law that just because evidence is really good, you don't need a warrant. That's almost what you are saying and you are losing me on that.

Counsel for the State: ... What I am saying is that because this really good evidence, this really probative evidence dissipates so quickly, at least in the case of heroin, and the public defender brought up some other drugs like marijuana and things like that, this is a whole different animal. I agree if this is a marijuana case, we would be done. We would be done because marijuana being a natural substance-cocaine being a natural substance-it doesn't break down. Heroin is a not natural substance-it's a synthetic and it does break down. That is why you need to get the evidence quickly. And that is why you have exigent circumstances because you need to get it quickly.

Justice Ziegler: So to be clear, you are basically asking us to revive Bohling in terms of heroin cases or substances that are not natural.

... [W]hat I really hear you saying is that in heroin cases there is an exigency because it dissipates so quickly. That's Bohling for heroin, isn't it?

¶ 74 The majority now asserts that "[w]e instead resolve this case 'based on its own facts and circumstances.'" Majority op. ¶ 42. Yet, all of the facts and circumstances the majority discusses relate only to dissipation: the type and amount of an ingested drug, the time it was ingested, the time it takes to get a warrant in relation to dissipation, and scientific evidence on the rapid dissipation of heroin. Id. Its best evidence rule places the focus on facts and circumstances relating only to dissipation. By inventing a best evidence rule for every heroin case and concluding that exigent circumstances exist because of the rapid dissipation of heroin, the majority creates a per se rule for heroin cases.

¶ 75 If the majority is correct that heroin is in the blood for only a few minutes and 6–monoacetylmorphine is present in the blood for only one to three hours before metabolizing into morphine, this would be the circumstance in every case. Even if the scientific evidence regarding the rate of dissipation changed, it would change for every case.

¶ 76 Likewise, the time it takes to obtain a warrant will always cause some delay in every case. In this case, Officer Fenhouse testified that that it takes approximately two hours to obtain a search warrant. Majority op. ¶ 14. However, McNeely sounds a note of caution, explaining that consideration of the time it takes to obtain a warrant "might well diminish the incentive for jurisdictions to pursue progressive approaches to warrant acquisition that preserve the protections afforded by the warrant while meeting the legitimate interests of law enforcement." McNeely, (citations omitted).

¶ 77 Underlying the majority's conclusion that the rate of dissipation of heroin in the blood justifies an exception to the warrant requirement is the majority's newly minted best evidence rule for heroin cases. According to the majority, "the officer could reasonably believe that waiting two hours to obtain a warrant would 'significantly undermin[e] the efficacy' of a blood draw by leading to ambiguous test results; evidence of heroin or morphine use, rather than heroin use alone, might result if sufficient time has passed." Majority op. ¶ 48.

¶ 78 The majority errs in its creation of a best evidence rule for heroin cases. It contradicts well-established law when it contends that a blood draw showing "heroin or its first metabolite, 6–monoacetylmorphine, remained the most probative evidence that Parisi had used heroin."[5] Majority Op. ¶ 46. "Neither Wisconsin law nor federal law recognizes a 'best evidence rule' that established a hierarchy of evidence. In effect, all evidence is created equal." 7 Daniel D. Blinka, Wisconsin Practice Series: Wisconsin Evidence (3rd ed.2008) (explaining the "myth of the best evidence rule").

¶ 79 Even if there were a best evidence rule, evidence of drugs in the bloodstream alone is not enough to support a possession charge. Here, Parisi was charged with possession of a schedule I or II narcotic drug. In Wisconsin, "the mere presence of drugs in a person's system is insufficient to prove that the drugs are knowingly possessed by the person or that the drugs are within the person's control." State v. Griffin (1998). Evidence of drugs in the bloodstream is "circumstantial evidence of prior possession" and must be "combined with other corroborating evidence of sufficient probative value" in order to prove possession. Id.

¶ 80 The majority's reasoning is flawed because even if the police had been able to detect heroin or its first metabolite 6–monoacetylmorphine in the bloodstream, they still would need corroborating evidence to convict Parisi of heroin possession. In this case, police found "a bindle of what looked to be heroin wrapped in tinfoil, some cut ends, and [a] marijuana pipe" at the scene of the overdose. Majority op. ¶ 10. Additionally, Parisi was given Narcan before he was transported to the hospital, which Officer Fenhouse knew was "usually administered for people who have overdosed on heroin." Majority op. ¶ 7. Thus, the heroin found in the apartment where Parisi overdosed and the fact that he was treated with Narcan present key corroborating evidence.

¶ 81 The majority's reliance on McNeely for support of a best evidence rule is misplaced. The term "best evidence" does not appear in the McNeely majority opinion. Additionally, there are distinctions between the presence of alcohol in the bloodstream and the presence of heroin.

¶ 82 Evidence of heroin or 6–monoacetylmorphine in the bloodstream is less probative than evidence of alcohol in the bloodstream because a BAC level alone is enough to obtain a drunk driving conviction. In contrast, evidence of drug use in the blood stream requires corroborating evidence for a possession conviction.

Moreover, the amount of alcohol in the blood is relevant to a conviction, but the amount of heroin in the blood is not. Unlike a BAC level, the police need find only a trace of heroin or its metabolites in the bloodstream.

¶ 83 In <u>State v. Jones</u>, the Nevada Supreme Court articulated this distinction. It determined that the dissipation of cocaine in the defendant's bloodstream was not an exigent circumstance that justified a departure from the normal procedure of obtaining a warrant. The <u>Jones</u> court explained that evidence of alcohol and drugs in the blood differ. <u>Id</u>. That analysis is applicable here: "a conviction for driving under the influence requires a specific minimum concentration of blood alcohol, whereas a conviction for being under the influence of a controlled substance requires only a trace amount of the substance or its metabolites." <u>Id.</u>

¶ 84 The majority also misunderstands <u>State v. Peardot</u>, (1984), when it cites to that case as support for the adoption of a best evidence rule. The term "best" was used merely as an adjective to describe the evidence. There is no discussion in <u>Peardot</u> supporting the adoption of a best evidence approach.

¶ 85 Finally, the majority's insistence that evidence of morphine in the bloodstream is less probative evidence than heroin or 6–monoacetylmorphine ignores the facts of this case. The warrantless blood draw performed on Parisi revealed evidence of morphine in his bloodstream, not heroin or 6–monoacetylmorphine. It is this very evidence of morphine in Parisi's bloodstream that the State seeks to use and Parisi seeks to suppress.

III.

¶ 86 Not only did <u>McNeely</u> reject a per se rule based on dissipation, it also set forth circumstances in which the police must obtain a warrant without exception. <u>McNeely</u> instructs that "where police officers can reasonably obtain a warrant before a blood sample can be drawn without significantly undermining the efficacy of the search, the Fourth Amendment mandates that they do so." <u>Id.; see also Tullberg.</u>

¶ 87 In a footnote, the majority rejects Parisi's arguments that a warrant should have been pursued because of the number of officers involved in the case. Majority op. ¶ 50 n. 15. It advances that "Officer Fenhouse could reasonably believe that asking another officer to obtain a warrant would be futile, given the short timeframe before evidence of heroin use disappeared." <u>Id.</u>

¶ 88 However, the <u>McNeely</u> court explained that in "a situation in which the warrant process will not significantly increase the delay before the blood test is conducted because an officer can take steps to secure a warrant while the suspect is being transported to a medical facility by another officer ... there would be no plausible justification for an exception to the warrant requirement." <u>Id.</u> at 1561. That is exactly the circumstance here, yet the majority's decision directly contravenes <u>McNeely</u>.

¶ 89 Under <u>McNeely</u>, there is no plausible justification for the majority's decision. It is undisputed that there were a total of five to seven officers working on Parisi's case. See majority op. ¶ 9. Officer Fenhouse and Officer Moua both followed Parisi's ambulance to the hospital. Majority op. ¶ 11. Any of the five to seven officers working on the case could have applied for a warrant while Officer Fenhouse followed Parisi to the hospital.

¶ 90 In addition, there was no reason for delay in obtaining a warrant given that the officers had probable cause as soon as they arrived at the scene. As referenced above, Parisi was given Narcan before he was transported to the hospital, which Officer Fenhouse knew was "usually administered for people who have overdosed on heroin." Majority op. ¶ 7. The officers at the scene also found "a bindle of what looked to be heroin wrapped in tinfoil, some cut ends, and [a] marijuana pipe." Majority op. ¶ 10.

¶ 91 There is also no explanation for the delay in obtaining a warrant once Officer Fenhouse arrived at the hospital. Although Officer Fenhouse intended to have Parisi's blood drawn immediately, Parisi was initially deemed to be too unstable for the procedure. During the two hours that Officer Fenhouse waited at the hospital before Parisi's blood could be drawn, there was nothing that prevented him from obtaining a warrant.

¶ 92 After McNeely, this court has allowed only one exception to the warrant requirement for blood draws based on exigent circumstances. Tullberg. The majority contends that Tullberg is an analogous case involving warrantless blood draws. Majority op. ¶¶ 30, 40. It is not.

¶ 93 At the outset, the Tullberg court noted that the investigating officer "did not improperly delay in obtaining a warrant. He did not have probable cause to believe that Tullberg operated the motor vehicle while under the influence of an intoxicant until nearly three hours after the accident. If anything, Tullberg's actions, rather than the deputy's, necessitated the warrantless blood draw."

¶ 94 In contrast to the facts of this case, only one deputy was initially dispatched to the chaotic scene of the fatal collision in Tullberg. Additionally, Tullberg was not at the scene of the collision and the investigating deputy did not know he was the driver. When he was finally interviewed at the hospital, Tullberg told the deputy that he was a passenger in the vehicle. It was not until nearly three hours after the collision when the investigation uncovered evidence that helped identify Tullberg as the driver responsible for the fatal collision.

¶ 95 Given the extraordinary facts and circumstances of that case, the Tullberg court explained that the deputy, when "confronted with such an accident scene and obstruction of his investigation, con- ducted himself reasonably." Under McNeely, and as it is applied in Tullberg, an exception to the warrant requirement for a blood draw is permissible only when circumstances prevent an officer from timely obtaining a warrant. Here, however, the majority's analysis focuses only on facts and circumstances relating to dissipation because there were no facts and circumstances preventing at least one of the five to seven officers from timely obtaining a warrant.

¶ 96 In its effort to excuse the multiple officers' inexplicable failure to obtain a warrant, the majority conflates dissipation in the bloodstream with cases involving the imminent destruction of physical evidence. See majority op. ¶ 50 n. 15. Relying on destruction of evidence cases, the majority asserts that "if officers suspect drugs are being flushed behind a closed door, [ ] the exigency is not eliminated merely because there are multiple officers at the scene." The majority then analogizes Officer Fenhouse's failure to obtain a warrant at the hospital to destruction of evidence cases where "split—second judgments—in circumstances that are tense, uncertain, and rapidly evolving."

¶ 97 Such reliance on destruction of evidence cases is unpersuasive, because "[t]he context of blood testing is different in critical respects from other destruction-of-evidence cases in which the police are truly confronted with a 'now or never' situation." McNeely, (1973). Dissipation of a substance in the blood differs from circumstances "in which the suspect has control over easily disposable evidence."

¶ 98 It is quite a stretch to compare the apparent availability of five to seven officers including a police officer sitting in a hospital waiting room for two hours, with a drug raid where officers hear evidence being flushed away. Likewise, the five to seven officers at the scene of the overdose knew that Parisi was not about to imminently destroy evidence. The police certainly did not have to break through the door on a moment's notice because Parisi's friends met the officers outside to help direct them to the proper location. Majority op. ¶ 5. When the police entered the apartment, Parisi was laying unresponsive on the living room floor in his own vomit. Majority op. ¶ 6. Unlike making a split-second decision to preserve evidence, the steady dissipation of heroin in the blood is just not the kind of emergency that justifies foregoing a warrant.

¶ 99 I determine that under the facts and circumstances of this case, one of the five to seven officers could have secured a warrant in the two and one-half hours before Parisi's blood was drawn without significantly undermining the efficacy of the search. Officers were dispatched to the scene at 12:38 a.m. and arrived five to ten minutes after dispatch. Majority op. ¶ 4. Shortly thereafter, Narcan, the antidote for heroin, was administered. Majority op. ¶ 7. The blood draw did not occur until 3:10 a.m. Majority op. ¶ 13.

¶ 100 The State has the burden of proving the existence of exigent circumstances. State v. Richter, 2000. It has utterly failed to do so here. Even if Officer Fenhouse's failure to seek a warrant is excusable—and it is not—there is a complete dearth of information as to why none of the available five to seven officers failed to seek a warrant.

¶ 101 Contrary to the majority, I conclude that there were no exigent circumstances justifying an exception to the warrant requirement. As a result, the warrantless blood draw violated Parisi's Fourth Amendment rights. Accordingly, I respectfully dissent.

¶ 102 I am authorized to state that Justice SHIRLEY S. ABRAHAMSON, J. joins this dissent.

1. How dangerous is it for users of illegal drugs to risk criminal charges?

2. Is the legal system overly complicated concerning drug-related criminal charges? Or is it overly simple?

EXCERPT FROM *THE TRAVELERS PROPERTY CASUALTY COMPANY OF AMERICA, ST. PAUL FIRE AND MARINE INSURANCE COMPANY, FEDERAL INSURANCE COMPANY AND GREAT NORTHERN INSURANCE COMPANY V. ANDA, INC. AND WATSON PHARMACEUTICALS, INC., V. GEMINI INSURANCE COMPANY*, FROM THE UNITED STATES DISTRICT COURT FOR THE SOUTHERN DISTRICT OF FLORIDA, AUGUST 26, 2016

Appeal from the United States District Court for the Southern District of Florida
Before WILLIAM PRYOR and JILL PRYOR, Circuit Judges, and STORY, District Judge.

[Honorable Richard W. Story, United States District Judge for the Northern District of Georgia, sitting by designation:]

This case involves an insurance coverage dispute arising out of a state court action seeking to hold Appellants liable for damages in connection with wide-spread prescription drug abuse in West Virginia. The district court held that Appellees have no duty to defend in the underlying action and granted summary judgment for Appellees. We affirm.

Defendants-Counter Plaintiffs-Appellants Anda, Inc. and Watson Pharmaceuticals, Inc. (collectively, "Anda") distribute pharmaceuticals. The State of West Virginia sued Anda and other pharmaceutical companies in West Virginia state court setting forth various causes of action related to the epidemic of prescription drug abuse and its costs to the State of West Virginia.

Anda purchased a number of general commercial liability insurance policies from Plaintiffs-Counter Defendants-Appellees The Travelers Property Casualty Company of America ("Travelers"), St. Paul Fire and Marine Insurance Company ("St. Paul"), Federal Insurance Company ("Federal"), and Great Northern Insurance Company ("Northern") and Counter Defendant-Appellee Gemini Insurance Company ("Gemini") (collectively, the "Insurers") between 2001 and 2013. Anda sought defense and indemnification in the West Virginia Action. The Insurers initiated this suit against Anda, seeking a declaratory judgment that they have no duty to defend or indemnify Anda in the underlying action in West Virginia state court. Federal and Gemini reached settlements with Anda on the eve of oral argument. Accordingly, we address only the issue of whether Anda is afforded coverage under the policies issued by Travelers and St. Paul. Because of the products exclusion clauses in those policies, we conclude that the policies provide no coverage for Anda.

I. BACKGROUND

Anda is a wholesale pharmaceutical distributor. The State of West Virginia has sued Anda and other pharmaceutical companies in West Virginia state court, requesting an injunction against their distribution practices and seeking compensation for expenses the state alleges it has incurred as a result of the proliferation of "Pill Mills" and the attendant "opioid epidemic." *State of West Virginia ex rel. Darrell V. McGraw Jr. v. Amerisourcebergen Drug Corp., et al.,* (the "West Virginia Action"). The State alleges that, as a result of Anda's conduct, it has been forced to dedicate significant resources to law enforcement and police operations, hospitals and emergency rooms, and jails and prisons. The costs imposed by the opioid epidemic have diverted funds that the State would have used for other purposes.

A. THE WEST VIRGINIA ACTION

The Amended Complaint in the West Virginia Action alleges that Anda and other pharmaceutical distributors are "an integral part of the Pill Mill process." The State alleges that pharmaceutical distributors, including Anda, knowingly or negligently flood the West Virginia market with commonly-abused drugs. The State claims that it has suffered myriad harms as a result of the over-supply of Anda's products in the market, the proliferation of Pill Mills, and the attendant opioid epidemic. Those harms include increased crime, congested hospitals and emergency rooms, exhausted law enforcement resources, overcrowded jails and prisons, and court dockets over-crowded with prescription drug-related cases and crimes committed by addicts. The State alleges that Anda's distribution of its products not only damages the health and safety of West Virginians, but also imposes massive economic damages on the State itself.

B. THE DECLARATORY JUDGMENT ACTION

The Insurers issued general commercial liability insurance policies to Anda between 2001 and 2013, with Traveler's and St. Paul's policies issuing between 2006 and 2013. Under these policies, the Insurers have the duty to defend and indemnify Anda in lawsuits seeking damages for or because of bodily injury. These policies exclude, however, coverage for damages included within products-completed provisions. The Travelers policy excludes coverage for injuries "arising out of" "[a]ny goods or products . . . manufactured, sold, handled, distributed[,] or disposed of by . . . You" (the "Travelers Products Exclusion"). Similarly, the St. Paul policy states: "We won't cover bodily injury or property damage that results from your products or completed work" (the "St. Paul Products Exclusion").

    The Insurers initiated the suit below, seeking a declaration that they have no duty to defend or indemnify Anda in the West Virginia Action. *Travelers Prop. Cas. Co. of Am. et al. v. Anda, Inc. et al.*, (S.D. Fla.). In an omnibus order deciding cross-motions for summary judgment, the district court concluded that because the State did not assert claims "for bodily injury" or "because of bodily injury," the

Travelers and St. Paul policies did not afford coverage. The district court found that the Travelers and St. Paul Products Exclusions were not triggered because no "bodily injury" was alleged. Anda moved for reconsideration of the court's grant of summary judgment for the Insurers. The district court denied that motion and this appeal followed.

II. STANDARD OF REVIEW

We review a district court's order granting a motion for summary judgment de novo. *Lindley v. F.D.I.C.*, (11th Cir. 2013). We may affirm the district court's judgment for any reason supported by the record, even if the court below did not rely upon the same reasoning. *See Williams v. Bd. of Regents*, (11th Cir. 2007).

III. DISCUSSION

In reaching its decision below, the district court relied on the policy language that required the insurers to defend or indemnify claims "because of" or "for" "bodily injury." *Travelers Prop. Cas. Co. of America, et al. v. Anda, Inc., et al.*, (Mar. 9, 2015). The district court concluded that the St. Paul and Travelers policies did not afford coverage because the State's Amended Complaint in the West Virginia Action asserted claims "for" and "because of" economic harm to the State rather than "bodily injury."

We decline to reach the question of whether the State's claims in the West Virginia Action are "for" or "because of" bodily injury. We think the better conclusion is that the St. Paul and Travelers policies do not afford coverage because of the policies' Products Exclusions.

The St. Paul and Travelers policies contain a "Products and Completed Work Exclusion" and a "Products Exclusion," respectively, that preclude coverage. Accordingly, St. Paul and Travelers have no duty to defend or indemnify.

The Travelers and St. Paul policies are general commercial liability policies that specifically exclude coverage for products liability. The Travelers Products Exclusion omits coverage for bodily injury "arising out of" Anda's products while the St. Paul Products Exclusion eliminates coverage for damage that "results from" Anda's products.

Each of these policies is governed by California law. California law interprets "arising out of" and "results from" similarly, and requires only a minimal causal connection or link between the products sold or distributed by an insured and the alleged injury. *Pension Trust Fund v. Fed. Ins. Co.*,(9th Cir. 2002) (collecting cases); *Cont'l Cas. Co. v. City of Richmond*, (9th Cir. 1985) ("'Arising out of' are words of much broader significance than 'caused by.' They are ordinarily understood to mean 'originating from,' 'having its origin in,' 'growing out of' or 'flowing from' or in short, 'incident to, or having a connection with.'").

The injuries alleged by the State in the West Virginia Action have, at the very minimum, a "connection with" Anda's products. In that action, the State seeks to enjoin the way Anda distributes its products. It also seeks monetary damages arising from the injuries—whether they be "bodily" or not—caused by these products. At bottom, the State claims that Anda and other pharmaceutical distributors have so flooded the market with their products that West Virginia suffers from an opioid epidemic. As a result of that epidemic, the State has suffered monetary losses that it now seeks to recover. The causal connection between Anda's products and the injuries alleged by the State is sufficient to meet the low bar set by California law. Accordingly, we conclude that all the underlying claims, if covered at all, are embraced within the Travelers and St. Paul Products Exclusions, which render any coverage inapplicable.

This holding is in line with our previous ruling in *Taurus Holdings, Inc. v. U.S. Fidelity and Guaranty Co.*, (11th Cir. 2004). In that case, we considered a question of insurance coverage for a similar underlying suit. There, government municipalities sued Taurus—which manufactures, sells, and distributes firearms—for expenses incurred as a result of gun violence in their communities. Taurus's commercial general liability insurance policies, like Anda's here, excluded coverage for damages included within a "products-completed operations hazard" provision. That provision similarly excluded coverage for "bodily injury and property damage . . . arising out of your product or your work." On appeal, we considered whether, under Florida law, the products-completed operations hazard exclusion applied to the underlying lawsuits against Taurus. We certified the question to the Florida Supreme Court, which held that the cost of medical and other services the municipalities incurred as a result of gun violence "arise out of" the use of guns. *Taurus Holdings, Inc. v. U.S. Fid. & Guar. Co.*, (Fla. 2005).

In so holding, the Florida Supreme Court defined the term "arising out of" broadly, meaning "'originating from,' 'having its origin in,' 'growing out of,' 'flowing from,' 'incident to' or 'having a connection with.'" (quoting *Hagen v. Aetna Cas. & Sur. Co.*, (Fla. 5th DCA 1996)). We conformed

CRITICAL PERSPECTIVES ON THE OPIOID EPIDEMIC

our holding in *Taurus* to the opinion of the Florida Supreme Court. We held that the products-completed operations hazard exclusion found in the commercial general liability policies Taurus purchased excluded coverage for the claims raised against Taurus in the underlying municipal suits. *Taurus Holdings, Inc. v. U.S. Fid. & Guar. Co.,* (11th Cir. 2005). The "arising out of" language in the Anda policy exclusions has the same meaning as that in the Taurus policies. As in *Taurus*, we interpret the exclusionary language here broadly and impose a low bar for causation. Accordingly, the commercial liability policies issued by Travelers and St. Paul exclude coverage for the claims raised against Anda in the West Virginia Action. The judgment of the district court is affirmed.

IV. CONCLUSION

We **AFFIRM** the summary judgment in favor of Travelers and St. Paul.

1. Who can be held responsible for the injuries people suffer from opioid use and abuse?

2. What sort of protection is offered by insurance, and who is being protected?

CHAPTER 4

WHAT THE ADVOCATES SAY

Doctors have noticed that they need to receive more than just automated warnings about the dangers of drug abuse whenever they prescribe opioids. They need relevant information that's useful when treating a particular patient, not just an automatic general warning.

In her group's study of automatic opioid drug alerts, which are generated by an electronic health record system whenever opioids were prescribed at an emergency room, Emma Genco observed that 98.9 percent of opioid alerts did not go on to prevent an "adverse drug event." After the doctors had treated 4,581 patients, Genco's group noticed that 14 adverse drug events were successfully prevented. But for every time an alert prevented an adverse event, healthcare providers at that emergency room also had to deal with more than 123 unnecessary alerts. "It is essential to refine clinical decision support alerting systems to eliminate inconsequential alerts to prevent alert fatigue and maintain patient safety," wrote Genco.[1] If doctors get too many unneeded alerts, they may get used to ignoring alerts — even the ones that are actually needed.

Instead of relying solely on alerts, it is perhaps best to diversify techniques for approaching opioid abuse. "Complementary and integrative approaches can have a positive impact in treating populations that suffer with opioid addiction," John Weeks, the editor of the *Journal of Alternative and Complementary Medicine*, notes.[2] There are many approaches to take when treating pain or injury, from massage and exercise therapies to music meditation and cognitive behavioral therapy, to name just a few of many techniques that don't use drugs. This is especially important in the United States, where Americans consume about 80 percent of the world's opioids although they make up 5 percent of the global population.

"TRENDS IN HEROIN USE IN EUROPE: WHAT DO TREATMENT DEMAND DATA TELL US?" FROM THE EUROPEAN MONITORING CENTRE FOR DRUGS AND DRUG ADDICTION (EMCDDA), MAY 2013

The current number of problem opioid users in Europe can be estimated at about 1.4 million, or 0.41 % of the adult population, with heroin being by far the most widely used opioid. Heroin use has developed along different timelines; several western European countries faced increases from the 1970s onward, whereas countries in Central and Eastern Europe saw a development in heroin use in the 1990s and later. Recent analyses of multiple indicators suggest that Europe may be witnessing a longer-term decline in heroin use, although countries show varying patterns and trends.

Understanding heroin use trends is a priority because of its public health impact; it is also a major challenge owing to several factors, including the relatively limited size of the population of users and their often poor health status and socioeconomic situation.

In this analysis, treatment demand data are explored to provide an insight into problem heroin use trends, while recognising that issues such as treatment coverage and relationships between incidence of drug use and treatment entry are very complex (Hickman et al., 2001) and need to be carefully considered.

DATA AND METHODS

The EMCDDA's treatment demand indicator (TDI) (EMCDDA, 2012a) collects information on the number and characteristics of people entering specialised drug treatment in Europe ([1]) and provides important insights into trends in problem drug use. Data are available for all clients entering treatment during a given year, as well as for the subgroup of those entering treatment for the very first time. In this analysis, TDI data were explored in order to assess changes over time in the number of people who have entered treatment for the first time in their life with heroin as the primary drug. ([2]) A trend analysis was performed for two time periods according to data availability: a 6-year period (2005–11) with data from 24 European countries and an 11-year period (2001–11) focusing on 15 European countries.

The analysis used the 'joinpoint regression method' (National Cancer Institute, 2011), which describes the direction and the magnitude of trends fitting various linear segments over the studied period. The method estimates the points in time when linear trend changes occur ('joinpoints'), without prior theoretical hypothesis. For the analysis, Europe was divided into two broad groups of countries (Western Europe and Eastern Europe) ([3]) in order to allow some examination of differences within the region (Barrio G. et al., 2013).

WHAT ARE THE TRENDS IN FIRST TREATMENT DEMAND FOR HEROIN USE?

Over the last decade, treatment demand data indicate an overall decrease in the number of people who have entered treatment for the first time for heroin-related problems.

Data from 15 countries ([4]) show a decrease from 33 000 to 28 000 heroin clients entering drug treatment for the first time over the period 2001–11. However, changing trends were reported over the period, with three different phases identified: (1) a decrease from 33 000 new heroin clients in 2001 to 27 000 in 2003, which represents a significant annual percentage change (APC) of –10% ([5]); (2) an increase from 27 000 to 34 000 new heroin clients between 2003 and 2007 (APC +5%); and (3) a decrease from 34 000 to 28 000 new heroin clients between 2007 and 2011 (APC –5%).

Based on a larger sample of countries, the period 2005–11 also shows an overall decrease in the number of heroin clients entering drug treatment for the first time but in two different phases. In the 24 European countries with available data ([6]), the number of first-time heroin clients increased from around 52 000 in 2005 to 61 000 in 2007 and then decreased to 42 000 in 2011. The pattern was observed in both geographical areas (Western and Eastern Europe), although the decrease started later in the east. Although no significant change is identified over the whole period, the period 2007–11 is characterised by a statistically significant decreasing APC of just under -12%. ([7]).

Overall trends mask differences between countries, and changes within countries over time. The following examples illustrate national variability regarding the extent and period of changes in the number of new heroin treatment demands. Bulgaria and the Czech Republic are both characterised by a decrease for the overall period 2001–11 (APC of just over -6% in both cases). In Spain, an initial significant decrease from 7 500 in 2001 to 4 000 new heroin clients in 2003 (APC -31%) was followed by a period of stability, no significant annual percentage change up or down, though the most recent data indicates an increase in numbers from 3 400 in 2009 to 4 500 in 2010. In the United Kingdom the figures show a decrease reported between 2001 and 2003 (from 16 000 to 15 000 new heroin clients) followed by an increase until 2006 (20 000 new heroin clients) ([8]), though the only significant trend identified was a significant annual decrease (APC -6%) between 2006 and 2011 (from 20 000 to 15 000 clients).

FACTS AND FIGURES

1.4 million the estimated number of problem opioid users in Europe. ([1])

10,000–20,000: the estimated number of opioid users dying each year from overdose, drug-related infectious diseases, violence and other causes.

400,000: the number of people entering specialised drug treatment in Europe; around half of whom have entered for the first time in their life.

10,000: treatment centers all over Europe reporting data on drug clients.

43 %: the proportion of drug clients entering treatment who have problems related to heroin use (26% of those entering treatment for the first time in their life).

44 %: the proportion of heroin clients injecting heroin as main route of administration (37% among new clients).

4 to 1: the ratio of male to female heroin clients.

35 years: the mean age of heroin clients at treatment entry.

22 years: the mean age at first heroin use.

([1]) Europe includes the 27 EU Member States, Croatia, Turkey and Norway. In some cases, data aren't available for all countries.

IS EUROPE'S HEROIN EPIDEMIC DECLINING?

Available data show a decrease in first treatment demand for heroin use in Europe between 2001 and 2011. Three shorter time periods have been identified with changes in trends. The findings have been confirmed by a 6-year trend assessment using a larger sample of countries.

A number of factors do warrant further investigation, in particular the rebound of first heroin treatment demands between 2003 and 2007 (Barrio et al., 2013). Uncertainties also derive from possible modification in contextual and methodological factors (i.e. treatment capacity, propensity to enter treatment, time lag to treatment, data-reporting coverage), which might have influenced the decrease in the number of new heroin clients over time (De la Fuente L., 2006; EMCDDA, 2012b; EMCDDA, 2012c).

Available information suggests however that the decrease in first treatment demand for heroin use – and indirectly in the incidence of problem heroin use – cannot be attributed to those elements for the following reasons: in the last decade, drug treatment in general and heroin treatment in particular have increased overall in Europe (EMCDDA, 2011); there are also no indications of changes in the propensity of heroin users entering treatment, and available information suggests that the time lag between first use and first treatment entry has not increased (Nordt C., 2009); and, finally, TDI data coverage (number of clients and of treatment centers covered) has also remained stable or has increased in most countries (EMCDDA, 2012b).

In this context, the main finding of this analysis confirms a decrease in first-time heroin treatment entrants for heroin use, which should reflect decreases in heroin initiation that occurred some years earlier ([9]). This decrease in incidence might have been due to several causes, which range from lack of interest among young people in a drug that is associated with very serious harms, to reductions in the availability of this drug in some markets. A decrease in the incidence of heroin use some years ago appears to be confirmed indirectly by other indicators, such as drug-induced deaths and heroin-related drug-law offences. Furthermore, information on heroin supply seems to indicate a decline in heroin availability (see box 'Heroin supply'), even if caution should be applied in interpreting these data and the relationship between changes in heroin market and in heroin use (EMCDDA, 2012b; EMCDDA, 2012c).

CONCLUSIONS

The analysis suggests fluctuations in first treatment demand for heroin use in Europe in the last decade, with significant declines since 2007. The raw numbers indicate this occurred earlier in western European countries than in countries in eastern Europe, and supports other analyses which highlight differing time trends in heroin epidemics in these regions. The most recent data, however, seem to suggest a tendency towards convergence across Europe as a whole. Bearing in mind the time lag between initiation of heroin use and heroin treatment demand (Nordt, C., 2010) a decline in incidence of heroin use is likely to have occurred some years earlier.

The decline in heroin use has important public health implications as it contributes to reductions in a range of serious health problems, including infections related to drug injection and overdose deaths. However, heroin trends need to be monitored actively and continuously, as past experience has shown that drug problems often come in epidemic waves, with new generations being exposed to risk, especially when they have limited knowledge and experience of the serious problems that use of heroin can cause (Barrio G. et al., 2013). Another issue to be taken into consideration is the use of other opioids, which has been reported by European countries and is now a major problem in other regions of the world, including North America.

HEROIN SUPPLY

The vast majority of the heroin available on European markets comes from south-west Asia, reflecting the fact that it is estimated that at least 80% of the global opium output originates from Afghanistan, with heroin manufacture occurring either there or in neighboring countries, such as Iran and Pakistan. With the exception of 2010, when a poppy blight affected the Afghan crop, annual opium global production has remained at historically high levels since 2006. Estimated heroin production (467 tonnes in 2011) has decreased significantly since 2006, however, reflecting the fact that it is now thought that a substantial part of the Afghan opium crop is not being processed into heroin (UNODC, 2012). It should be also noted that estimation in this area is challenging and current approaches are under review.

Heroin has predominantly been transported from south-west Asia to Europe by two distinct routes. Historically, the less important of these has been the 'northern' or 'silk' route, which goes via the Central Asian Republics and then into Russia, Belarus and Ukraine. The 'Balkan route' is generally considered more important and runs principally through Turkey and the Balkan countries branching from there to southern, central and northern Europe.

Quantities of heroin seized in Europe (13.4 tonnes in 2011) are decreasing. This is a relatively long-term trend, which can be observed for a decade or more in the EU. The situation in Turkey is somewhat different. This country now seizes more heroin than all EU Member States, although seizures have significantly declined since a peak year in 2009. This reversal in Turkey may reflect changes in both trafficking flows and law enforcement activity. Law enforcement cooperation, both with countries in the region and with destination countries, appears to have made an impact, possibly resulting in a diversification of trafficking routes and modi operandi. More attention may now be given to the northern route, and new land, sea and air transport routes and methods appear to be being utilised. This includes using both airfreight and sea containers from countries such as Pakistan. Transit points on the Arabian peninsula and in east and west Africa also appear to be growing in importance. There are reports that some traffickers are moving to other illicit cargoes, such as contraband cigarettes, cannabis or cocaine, in preference to heroin. Whether this is driven by supply reduction activities, reduced market demand or a combination of both remains unclear.

1. If there is a decrease in the amount of heroin available will that force a decline in the use of such opioids?

2. What other facts can cause a decrease in the number of persons using a particular kind of opioid?

EXCERPT FROM *THE PRESCRIPTION OPIOID EPIDEMIC: AN EVIDENCE-BASED APPROACH*, EDITED BY G. C. ALEXANDER, S. FRATTAROLI, AND A. C. GIELEN, FROM THE JOHNS HOPKINS BLOOMBERG SCHOOL OF PUBLIC HEALTH, NOVEMBER 2015

EXECUTIVE SUMMARY

Prescription drugs are essential to improving the quality of life for millions of Americans living with acute or chronic pain.

However, misuse, abuse, addiction, and overdose of these products, especially opioids, have become serious public health problems in the United States. A comprehensive response to this crisis must focus on preventing new cases of opioid addiction, identifying early opioid-addicted individuals, and ensuring access to effective opioid addiction treatment while safely meeting the needs of patients experiencing pain.

At the invitation of the Johns Hopkins Bloomberg School of Public Health and the Clinton Foundation, a diverse group of experts were convened to chart a path forward to address these issues. After a town hall meeting at the School, featuring an inspiring call to action from President Bill Clinton[1], the group — including clinicians, researchers, government officials, injury prevention professionals, law enforcement leaders, pharmaceutical manufacturers and distributers, lawyers, health insurers and patient representatives — spent the next day and a half:

- Reviewing what is known about prescription opioid misuse, abuse, addiction and overdose;
- Identifying strategies for reversing the alarming trends in injuries, addiction, and deaths from these drugs; and
- Making recommendations for action.

Following this meeting, the group released a consensus statement with three guiding principles for translating the meeting discussion into actionable recommendations.[2]

INFORMING ACTION WITH EVIDENCE.

Some evidence-based interventions exist to inform action to address this public health emergency; these should be scaled up and widely disseminated. Furthermore, many promising ideas are evidence-informed, but have not yet been rigorously evaluated.

The urgent need for action requires that we rapidly implement and carefully evaluate these promising policies and programs.

The search for new, innovative solutions also needs to be supported.

INTERVENING COMPREHENSIVELY.

We support approaches that intervene all along the supply chain, and in the clinic, community and addiction treatment settings. Interventions aimed at stopping individuals from progressing down a pathway that will lead to misuse, abuse, addiction and overdose are needed. Effective primary, secondary and tertiary prevention strategies are vital. The importance of creating synergies across different interventions to maximize available resources is also critical.

PROMOTING APPROPRIATE AND SAFE USE OF PRESCRIPTION OPIOIDS.

Used appropriately, prescription opioids can provide relief to patients. However, these therapies are often being prescribed in quantities and for conditions that are excessive, and in many cases, beyond the evidence base. Such practices, and the lack of attention to safe use, storage and disposal of these drugs, contribute to the misuse, abuse, addiction and overdose increases that have occurred over the past decade. We support efforts to maximize the favorable risk/benefit balance of prescription opioids by optimizing their use in circumstances supported by best clinical practice guidelines.

Meeting participants formed seven working groups to make recommendations on: 1) prescribing guidelines, 2) prescription drug monitoring programs, 3) pharmacy benefit managers and pharmacies, 4) engineering strategies, 5) overdose education and naloxone distribution programs, 6) addiction treatment, and 7) community-based prevention.

RECOMMENDATIONS FOR ACTION

#1 PRESCRIBING GUIDELINES

1.1 Repeal existing permissive and lax prescription laws and rules.

1.2 Require oversight of pain treatment.

1.3 Provide physician training in pain management and opioid prescribing and establish a residency in pain medicine for medical school graduates.

#2: PRESCRIPTION DRUG MONITORING PROGRAMS (PDMPS)

2.1 Mandate prescriber PDMP use.

2.2 Proactively use PDMP data for enforcement and education purposes.

2.3 Authorize third-party payers to access PDMP data with proper protections.

2.4 Empower licensing boards for health professions and law enforcement to investigate high-risk prescribers and dispensers.

#3: PHARMACY BENEFIT MANAGERS (PBMS) AND PHARMACIES

3.1 Inform and support evaluation research.

3.2 Engage in consensus process to identify evidence-based criteria for using PBM and pharmacy claims data to identify people at high risk for abuse and in need of treatment.

3.3 Expand access to Prescription Drug Monitoring Programs.

3.4 Improve management and oversight of individuals who use controlled substances.

3.5 Support restricted recipient (lock-in) programs.

3.6 Support take-back programs.

3.7 Improve monitoring of pharmacies, prescribers and beneficiaries.

3.8 Incentivize electronic prescribing.

#4: ENGINEERING STRATEGIES

4.1 Convene a stakeholder meeting to assess the current product environment (e.g., products available, evidence to support effectiveness, regulatory issues) and identify high-priority future directions for engineering-related solutions.

4.2 Sponsor design competitions to incentivize innovative packaging and dispensing solutions.

4.3 Secure funding for research to assess the effectiveness of innovative packaging and designs available and under development.

4.4 Use research to assure product uptake.

#5: OVERDOSE EDUCATION AND NALOXONE DISTRIBUTION PROGRAMS

5.1 Engage with the scientific community to assess the research needs related to naloxone distribution evaluations and identify high-priority future directions for naloxone-related research.

5.2 Partner with product developers to design naloxone formulations that are easier to use by nonmedical personnel and less costly to deliver.

5.3 Work with insurers and other third-party payers to ensure coverage of naloxone products.

5.4 Partner with community-based overdose education and naloxone distribution programs to identify stable funding sources to ensure program sustainability.

5.5. Engage with the healthcare professional community to advance consensus guidelines on the co-prescription of naloxone with prescription opioids.

#6: ADDICTION TREATMENT

6.1 Invest in surveillance of opioid addiction.

6.2 Expand access to buprenorphine treatment.

6.3 Require federally-funded treatment programs to allow patients access to buprenorphine or methadone.

6.4 Provide treatment funding for communities with high rates of opioid addiction and limited access to treatment.

6.5 Develop and disseminate a public education campaign about the important role for treatment in addressing opioid addiction.

6.6 Educate prescribers and pharmacists about how to prevent, identify and treat opioid addiction.

6.7 Support treatment-related research.

#7: COMMUNITY-BASED PREVENTION STRATEGIES

7.1 Invest in surveillance to ascertain how patients in treatment for opioid abuse and those who have overdosed obtain their supply.

7.2 Convene a stakeholder meeting with broad representation to create guidance that will help communities undertake comprehensive approaches that address the supply of, and demand for, prescription opioids in their locales; implement and evaluate demonstration projects that model these approaches.

7.3 Convene an inter-agency task force to ensure that current and future national public education campaigns about prescription opioids are informed by the available evidence and that best practices are shared.

7.4 Provide clear and consistent guidance on safe storage of prescription drugs.

7.5 Develop clear and consistent guidance on safe disposal of prescription drugs; expand access to take-back programs.

7.6 Require that federal support for prescription drug misuse, abuse and overdose interventions include outcome data.

BACKGROUND

In May 2014, a diverse group of experts — including clinicians, researchers, government officials, injury prevention professionals, law enforcement leaders, pharmaceutical manufacturers and distributers, lawyers, health insurers and patient representatives — gathered at the Johns Hopkins Bloomberg School of Public Health. The group gathered to review what is known about prescription opioid misuse, abuse, addiction and overdose; to identify strategies for reversing the alarming trends in injuries and deaths from these drugs; and to make recommendations for action. The group convened at the invitation of the Clinton Foundation and two of the School's centers: the John Hopkins Center for Drug Safety and Effectiveness and the John Hopkins Center for Injury Research and Policy. Prior to the meeting, the School hosted a public town hall meeting during which President Bill Clinton provided an inspiring call to action.

During the day-and-a-half meeting, participants identified opportunities for intervention along the supply chain (including the development and production process, legal and illegal markets, and insurance coverage); and within the clinical, community and addiction treatment settings. The result was a commitment to develop and implement a plan of action that utilizes the multidisciplinary skills and expertise of the many stakeholders committed to addressing the issue.

In the months that followed this initial gathering, the group divided into work groups to review the available evidence and make recommendations based on that literature. This process was guided by the following principles:

INFORMING ACTION WITH EVIDENCE.

Some evidence-based interventions exist to inform action to address this public health emergency; these should be scaled up and widely disseminated. Furthermore, many promising ideas are evidence-informed, but have not yet been rigorously evaluated. The urgent need for action requires that we rapidly implement and carefully evaluate these promising policies and programs. The search for new, innovative solutions also needs to be supported.

INTERVENING COMPREHENSIVELY.

We support approaches that intervene all along the supply chain, and in the clinic, community and addiction treatment settings. Interventions aimed at stopping individuals from progressing down a pathway that will lead to misuse, abuse, addiction and overdose are needed. Effective primary, secondary and tertiary prevention strategies are vital. The importance of creating synergies across different interventions to maximize available resources is also critical.

PROMOTING APPROPRIATE AND SAFE USE OF PRESCRIPTION OPIOIDS.

Used appropriately, prescription opioids can provide relief to patients. However, these therapies are often being prescribed in quantities and for conditions that are excessive, and in many cases, beyond the evidence base. Such practices, and the lack of attention to safe use, storage and disposal of these drugs, contribute to the misuse, abuse, addiction and overdose increases that have occurred over the past decade. We support efforts to maximize the favorable risk/benefit balance of prescription opioids by optimizing their use in circumstances supported by best clinical practice guidelines. This report is the result of the work group process.

OVERVIEW

Prescription drugs are essential to improving the functioning and quality of life for patients living with acute or chronic medical conditions. Although all prescription drugs have some misuse risk, of particular concern is the misuse and abuse of the drugs identified by the Drug Enforcement Administration (DEA) as controlled substances. These products, such as prescription opioids, have high abuse potential and can lead to life-threatening adverse events when taken in excess or in combination with other drugs.[1,2]

Prescription drug abuse and overdose is a serious public health problem in the United States. Drug overdose death rates in the U.S. increased five-fold between 1980 and 2008, making drug overdose the leading cause of injury death.[3] In 2013, opioid analgesics were involved in 16,235 deaths — far exceeding deaths from any other drug or drug class, licit or illicit.[4] According to the National Survey on Drug Use and Health (NSDUH), in 2012 an estimated 2.1 million Americans were addicted to opioid pain relievers and 467,000 were addicted to heroin.[5] These estimates do not include an additional 2.5 million or more pain patients who may be suffering from an opioid use disorder because the NSDUH excludes individuals receiving legitimate opioid prescriptions.[6]

A public health response to this crisis must focus on preventing new cases of opioid addiction, early identification of opioid-addicted individuals, and ensuring access to effective opioid addiction treatment, while at the same time continuing to safely meet the needs of patients experiencing pain. It is widely recognized that a multi-pronged approach is needed to address the prescription opioid epidemic. A successful response to this problem will target the points along the spectrum of prescription drug production, distribution, prescribing, dispensing, use and treatment that can contribute to abuse; and offer opportunities to intervene for the purpose of preventing and treating misuse, abuse and overdose.

This report provides a comprehensive overview of seven target points of opportunity, summarizes the evidence about intervention strategies for each, and offers recommendations for advancing the field through policy and practice.

#1: Prescribing Guidelines

#2: Prescription Drug Monitoring Programs

#3: Pharmacy Benefit Managers and Pharmacies

#4: Engineering Strategies

#5: Overdose Education and Naloxone Distribution Programs

#6: Addiction Treatment

#7: Community-Based Prevention

1. How can meetings among people with diverse responsibilities result in not only recommendations, but concrete actions for addiction healthcare?

EXCERPT FROM "THE OPIOID SURVEY," FROM THE INTERNATIONAL ADHESIONS SOCIETY, MARCH 29, 2013

1. SUMMARY

The International Adhesions Society (IAS) provides information, advocacy, support and research for patients and families suffering from adhesions, abnormal fibrous tissue connections caused by surgery or disease such as infection or endometriosis. Abdomino-pelvic adhesions patients may develop a syndrome which makes them practically indistinguishable from those diagnosed with interstitial cystitis, dyspareunia, IBS, or lower back pain. The 15-25 million US patients suffering with these conditions experience chronic, unrelenting pain often treated with opioids.

Opioid use must be understood in the wider context of pain. Chronic pain affects over 100 million Americans, costing $560-635 billion yearly in medical expenses and productivity. The inestimable human cost of addiction and death caused by opioids is part of the larger tragedy of unrelieved chronic pain. Opioids, alone or combined with other drugs account for about 75% of deaths due to prescription drugs. Opioid sales are about $9 billion but societal costs of opioid abuse and misuse were estimated (2007) at $56 billion, almost double the 2012 appropriation for NIH, 158 times its budget for chronic pain research and only 30% less than the Federal budget sequester.

After implementing a strategy to mitigate the risks of abuse and misuse of some opioid formulations, FDA is considering limits on indications for the type and severity of pain, and dose and duration of treatment for all opioids.

None of our patients want to take pain medications. We are concerned that the proposals will precipitate a "cold turkey" for millions of chronic pain patients. An integrated policy must be implemented to wean the nation from opioids by funding and developing alternatives such as the one we have evaluated for pelvic pain[1] – PainShield® MD Therapeutic Ultrasound – and found to reduce opioid use in some patients. Accordingly, we wish to:

- Ensure access to adequate pain relief for chronic pain patients.
- State why the proposals lack scientific basis, will reduce access to analgesia and are unlikely to succeed.
- Present our own data, generated specifically in response to FDA's request regarding this issue, involving 2840 patients representative of, conservatively, 30 million Americans with chronic pain related to pelvic, abdominal & spinal adhesions, endometriosis, interstitial cystitis and related conditions. Our data highlight concerns that the proposals will reduce the ability of a large majority (>80%) of these patients to access pain medication or to be reimbursed for it. In these patients, the use of opioids:

- exceeds 90 days (85.5%), and often more than 2 years (54.8% of patients).
- sometimes exceeds 100mg morphine equivalent daily (24.3% of patients).
- treats pain that is less than severe (46.3%).
- is necessary, even with non-severe pain because other approaches have failed to provide relief.
- would be regarded as "off-label" in 92.4% of patients if the labeling proposals are implemented.

- Highlight flaws in the approach of FDA and other agencies to this problem, and to propose revisions to:
  - Challenge paradigms that drugs are the modality and opioids are the analgesics of choice.
  - Formulate a coordinated national strategy to deal with prescription drug abuse and misuse.
  - Define FDA's role in these national efforts without compromising its primary mission.
- Expedite a national strategy on pain prevention, treatment, management, and research, which includes the development of, and access to, pharmaceutical and non- pharmaceutical alternatives to opioid analgesia.

1. Who benefits from research into alternative pain therapy?

2. What alternative pain therapies are available in your community?

"A NEW ABUSE-DETERRENT OPIOID – XTAMPZA ER," BY THE EDITORS OF *THE MEDICAL LETTER ON DRUGS AND THERAPEUTICS*, JUNE 20, 2016

[*Editor's note: Tables are not included in this reprint and can be found with the original article.*]

The FDA has approved *Xtampza ER* (Collegium), a new extended-release, abuse-deterrent capsule formulation of oxycodone, for management of pain severe enough to require daily, around-the-clock, long-term opioid treatment and for which alternative treatment options are inadequate.

ABUSE-DETERRENT OPIOIDS — Five other abuse-deterrent opioid formulations were approved earlier, three as single-drug products and two in combinations with opioid antagonists.[1] Two of these products, *Morphabond* (morphine ER) and *Targiniq ER* (oxycodone ER/naloxone), have not yet been marketed. *Zohydro ER* (hydrocodone ER) was reformulated in 2015 to make abuse more difficult, but it has not received FDA approval as an abuse-deterrent opioid. No studies are available comparing the relative safety of these products.

No opioid formulation prevents consumption of a large number of intact dosage units, the most common method of abuse. Abuse-deterrent formulations have one or more properties that make their intentional non-therapeutic use more difficult, less attractive, or less rewarding.

THE NEW FORMULATION — *Xtampza ER* is available in capsules containing microspheres formulated with oxycodone base and inactive ingredients that make the formulation more difficult to manipulate for the purpose of abuse. Each capsule

131

contains 9, 13.5, 18, 27, or 36 mg of oxycodone (equivalent to 10, 15, 20, 30 or 40 mg of oxycodone HCl, respectively).

PHARMACOKINETICS — The oral bioavailability of *Xtampza ER* is greater when taken with food (Cmax increased by 100-150% and AUC by 50-60% with a high-fat meal). In one pharmacokinetic study, crushing *Xtampza ER* capsules did not increase the Cmax or the AUC of oxycodone compared to intact capsules when both were taken with a high-fat meal. Crushing the capsules also did not compromise the extended-release properties of *Xtampza ER*, unlike *OxyContin* abuse-deterrent tablets, which lost their extended-release properties when crushed.[2] In another study, crushing and snorting *Xtampza ER* capsules following a high-fat meal resulted in lower peak serum concentrations of oxycodone than taking intact capsules.[3]

CLINICAL STUDIES — A 12-week, randomized, double-blind trial in 740 patients with moderate to severe chronic low back pain compared *Xtampza ER* with placebo. The maximum dose was 144 mg/day (equivalent to 160 mg of oxycodone HCl). Patients treated with the active drug had significantly lower pain scores from week 2-12 than those who received placebo.[4]

ADVERSE EFFECTS — Nausea, headache, constipation, somnolence, pruritus, vomiting, and dizziness, all typical opioid side effects, occurred commonly in the clinical trial in patients treated with *Xtampza ER*.

PREGNANCY — As with other opioid analgesics, prolonged use of *Xtampza ER* during pregnancy can cause neonatal opioid withdrawal syndrome. Oxycodone is excreted in breast milk and can cause opioid effects in breastfed newborns.

DRUG INTERACTIONS — Oxycodone is metabolized mainly by CYP3A4 and to a lesser extent by CYP2D6. Administration of *Xtampza ER* concurrently with drugs that inhibit CYP3A4 (or discontinuation of CYP3A4 inducers) can increase serum concentrations of oxycodone and could be fatal. Concurrent use of CYP3A4 inducers could decrease oxycodone serum concentrations and the analgesic effect of the drug.[5]

DOSAGE AND ADMINISTRATION — The recommended starting dosage of *Xtampza ER* for opioid-naive patients is 9 mg every 12 hours. The capsules must be taken with food; patients should consume the same amount of food with every dose in order to ensure consistent plasma levels. For patients who have difficulty swallowing the capsules, their contents can be sprinkled on soft foods or into a cup, and then given orally or through a gastrostomy or nasogastric tube. The maximum daily dose of *Xtampza ER* is 288 mg (equivalent to 320 mg oxycodone HCl). The package insert contains dosing instructions for conversion from other oxycodone formulations or other opioids. Patients with hepatic impairment starting *Xtampza ER* should take one-third to one-half the usual dosage; they should not take the drug if the required dose is <9 mg. Patients should be monitored for respiratory depression for 72 hours after either starting treatment or increasing the dose.

CONCLUSION — *Xtampza ER* is the second extended-release abuse-deterrent formulation of oxycodone. How it compares to the abuse-deterrent formulation of *OxyContin* for prevention of misuse is unknown. Whether use of abuse-deterrent opioid products actually reduces overall opioid abuse remains to be determined.

Reprinted with special permission from The Medical Letter on Drugs and Therapeutics, June 20, 2016; Vol. 58 (1497):77-78.

1. What are placebos and why do they work at all?

2. Why are medical manufacturers studying new pain medications instead of placebos?

"AAN: RISKS OF OPIOIDS OUTWEIGH BENEFITS FOR HEADACHE, LOW BACK PAIN, OTHER CONDITIONS," FROM THE AMERICAN ACADEMY OF NEUROLOGY, SEPTEMBER 29, 2014

© 2014 American Academy of Neurology. Reproduced with permission.

MINNEAPOLIS – According to a new position statement from the American Academy of Neurology (AAN), the risk of death, overdose, addiction or serious side effects with prescription opioids outweigh the benefits in chronic, non-cancer conditions such as headache, fibromyalgia and chronic low back pain. The position paper is published in the September 30, 2014, print issue of *Neurology*, the medical journal of the American Academy of Neurology. Opioids, or narcotics, are pain medications including morphine, codeine, oxycodone, methadone, fentanyl, hydrocodone or a combination of the drugs with acetaminophen.

"More than 100,000 people have died from prescription opioid use since policies changed in the late 1990s to allow much more liberal long-term use," said Gary M. Franklin, MD, MPH, research professor in the Department of Environmental & Occupational Health Sciences in the University of Washington School of Public Health in Seattle and a Fellow with the AAN. "There have been more deaths from prescription opioids in the most vulnerable young to middle-aged groups than from firearms and car accidents. Doctors, states, institutions and patients need to work together to stop this epidemic."

Studies have shown that 50 percent of patients taking opioids for at least three months are still on opioids five years later. A review of the available studies showed that while opioids may provide significant short-term pain relief, there is no substantial evidence for maintaining pain relief or improved function over long periods of time without serious risk of overdose, dependence or addiction. The AAN recommends that doctors consult with a pain management specialist if dosage exceeds 80 to 120 (morphine-equivalent dose) milligrams per day, especially if pain and function have not substantially improved in their patients. The statement also provides the following suggestions for doctors to prescribe opioids more safely and effectively:

- Create an opioid treatment agreement
- Screen for current or past drug abuse
- Screen for depression
- Use random urine drug screenings
- Do not prescribe medications such as sedative-hypnotics or benzodiazepines with opioids
- Assess pain and function for tolerance and effectiveness
- Track daily morphine equivalent dose using an online dosing calculator

- Seek help if the morphine-equivalent dose reaches 80 to 120 milligrams and pain and function have not substantially improved
- Use the state Prescription Drug Monitoring Program to monitor all prescription drugs the patient may be taking

"More research and information regarding opioid effectiveness and management is needed, along with changes in state and federal laws and policy to ensure that patients are safer when prescribed these drugs," said Franklin. To learn more about painful brain and nervous system disorders, please visit www.aan.com/patients.

The American Academy of Neurology is the world's largest association of neurologists and neuroscience professionals, with 30,000 members. The AAN is dedicated to promoting the highest quality patient-centered neurologic care. A neurologist is a doctor with specialized training in diagnosing, treating and managing disorders of the brain and nervous system such as Alzheimer's disease, stroke, migraine, multiple sclerosis, concussion, Parkinson's disease and epilepsy.

For more information about the American Academy of Neurology, visit AAN.com or find us on Facebook, Twitter, LinkedIn and YouTube.

1. How can working people in the prime of life be vulnerable to opioid addiction?

2. What can doctors do to prevent such opioid dependency in their patients?

"HEALTH ADVOCATES: TO COMBAT OPIOID EPIDEMIC, TARGET BIG PHARMA," BY NADIA PRUPIS, FROM *COMMON DREAMS*, SEPTEMBER 17, 2015

Faced with a growing nationwide opioid addiction, health and consumer advocates say it's time to identify and sever ties with the culprits behind the scourge—pain medication manufacturers and the companies who promote their products.

In Massachusetts, which recently saw a spike in deaths related to heroin overdoses, police and community organizations in Gloucester implemented a new program this year—known as the Angel Initiative—to help addicts get clean in favor of arresting them for illegal drug use.

But on Wednesday, the Gloucester police force added a new effort to the initiative: laying bare the links between opioid abuse and the country's largest pharmaceutical companies.

In a widely-shared Facebook post, the department listed the contact information of chief executives of Eli Lilly, Abbott Labs, Merck, Johnson & Johnson, and Pfizer and encouraged its followers to "politely ask them what they are doing to address the opioid epidemic in the United States and if they realize that the latest data shows almost 80% of addicted persons start with a legally prescribed drug that they make."

For their part, police said, they would make the same calls.

The salvo came on the same day as consumer advocacy group Public Citizen issued a letter to Congress urging lawmakers to publicize financial ties between medication manufacturers and their promoters, stating that they "may be responsible for the increasing epidemic of pain medication addiction and overdose deaths by promoting misleading information about the medications' safety and effectiveness."

Dr. Andrew Kimby, executive director of Physicians for Responsible Opioid Prescribing and one of the letter's signatories, explained, "By promoting opioid use for common problems, drug makers and their proxies ushered in an addiction epidemic that will take decades for our country to recover from."

The Senate Finance Committee in 2012 launched an investigation into three pharmaceutical companies and seven nonprofit organizations—prompted by evidence that growing opioid addiction came after aggressive marketing of pain medication—and has yet to release its findings, Public Citizen noted.

"The results of the investigation are not simply a matter of historical importance," said Dr. Michael Carome, director of Public Citizen's Health Research group. "They are crucial to saving lives because these groups continue promoting aggressive opioid use and continue blocking federal and state interventions that could reduce overprescribing."

Another of the signatories is Judy Rummler, chair of the Fed Up! Coalition, an alliance of grassroots organizations fighting to end the opioid addiction epidemic, who lost her son Steve to an opioid overdose from legally prescribed medication. Rummler called on Congress to release the results of the investigation, which she said "will make it harder for these pain groups to keep claiming their efforts are on behalf of patients."

"The prescribing practices they promote are hurting many chronic pain sufferers, not helping them," Rummler said.

Many in Gloucester said they would follow the police department's lead in contacting the executives of the pharmaceutical companies. "The war on drugs should always have been against big Pharma," said one commenter. "They are the real drug dealers but they line too many pockets with too much."

1. Do you think that drug makers should be held accountable for their role in the opioid epidemic? Why or why not?

2. Do you agree with the statement in the final paragraph of this article, that so-called Big Pharma are "the real drug dealers" in the opioid epidemic?

"SUBSTANCE-ABUSE TREATMENT INDUSTRY GROWS TO KEEP UP WITH DEMAND," BY COURTNEY COLUMBUS, FROM *CRONKITE NEWS*, JANUARY 5, 2017

TUCSON – At 19, Joey Romeo had his wisdom teeth removed.

His doctor prescribed 180 pills of hydromorphone, an opioid, to relieve the pain. That triggered a cascade of events that would take him in and out of more than 10 addiction treatment programs in two states.

Romeo, now 25, had tried prescription drugs before. But his mother, Susan Romeo, said after the 180-pill prescription, "There was no going back. He was 100 percent addicted."

Romeo and his family have accumulated hundreds of thousands of dollars in bills trying to get him off — and keep him off — the pills. His parents have paid insurance copays for Joey's time at addiction treatment centers. They have paid for stays in sober living homes. And they have paid Joey's bills while he looks for jobs.

Susan keeps a crate full of the bills, pulling out stacks of them and piling them on the dining room table in her Tucson home.

"I don't even count it. I would cry," Susan said. "If I added up all the numbers, I'd probably be beside myself because I don't want to think about it."

Cronkite News conducted a four-month investigation into the rise of prescription opioid abuse in Arizona. Dozens of journalists at Arizona State University examined thousands of records and traveled across the state to interview addicts, law enforcement, public officials and health care experts. The goal: uncover the root of the epidemic, explain the ramifications and provide solutions.

Since 2010, more than 3,600 people have overdosed and died from opioids in Arizona. In 2015, the dead numbered 701 — the highest of any year before, or nearly two per day, according to an analysis by the Arizona Department of Health Services.

As the opioid epidemic continues to affect more Americans every year, the substance-abuse treatment industry has grown to keep up with demand. Americans spent $34 billion on substance use disorder treatment in 2014, up from $9 billion in 1986, according to the Substance Abuse and

Mental Health Services Administration, a Maryland-based federal agency that aims to improve behavioral health.

It's difficult to determine the exact number of facilities that provide opioid-addiction treatment in Arizona because the state has varying degrees of regulation. For example, state officials don't track unlicensed facilities, such as sober living homes, which don't provide medical treatment. However, there are at least 650 licensed treatment providers in the state.

Those within the industry say they've noticed new rehab centers opening in Arizona. Not only are more people becoming addicted, the powerful effect of opioids on the brain makes it common for recovering addicts to relapse – meaning more time in rehab centers and more money out the door.

Experts say the high cost at some facilities, wait lists for centers that accept state-funded health plans, differences in quality of care and a complicated mix of treatment options mean it's often difficult for addicts in Arizona to access effective care.

Angie Geren, executive director of the nonprofit Addiction Haven and a clinician at a Community Medical Services methadone clinic in Phoenix, helps to guide the families of recovering addicts through the treatment center system.

"Our treatment industry is so splintered. It's so hard for parents," she said. "No one has a road map of where to go."

INDUSTRY GROWTH

Since 1999, the amount of opioids prescribed by doctors in the U.S. nearly quadrupled, but the overall amount of pain reported stayed the same, according to the Centers for Disease Control and Prevention.

"Given the scope of the epidemic, you only have about 20 percent of opioid-addicted people in treatment," said Mark Parrino of the American Association for the Treatment of Opioid Dependence, a New York-based organization founded in 1984 that works to increase access to opioid treatment programs.

Still, the number of patients the group says has received care at opioid treatment programs has grown by 75,000 in the past 10 years.

Access to these centers varies across states and between urban and rural locations and often depends on each state's laws and available public funding.

IBISWorld, an industry research firm, estimated the mental health and substance abuse industry would continue to grow during the next five years because of rising incomes and better insurance coverage.

And, opioid addicts tend to relapse several times.

Jeff Wondoloski, a therapist at Valley Hope of Chandler, said it can be especially easy for youth to relapse.

"When you take them off drugs, when you help them get sober, what happens is they pick up where they left off when they started using," he said. "So you have someone who's 24 who has the maturation of a 13, 14 year old. They're lost, you know. There isn't a whole lot of programs that are helping those individuals long term."

He said the youth he works with tend to go through treatment more times than people in their 40s or 50s.

"You hear these young people talking about – almost bragging about – how many treatment centers they've been to, how many overdoses they've had, how many times they've had to get (opiate antidote) Narcan," Wondoloski said. "You know, it's like this badge of honor almost, and that's sad."

The substance abuse administration estimates that about two thirds of the money spent on treatment in 2014 came from public funds, while the remaining $11 billion was private spending.

Fair Health, a national nonprofit group, analyzed the costs of opioid abuse and dependence treatment. It found the number of private insurance claims submitted for opiate dependence had skyrocketed 3,200 percent from 2007 to 2014.

COST OF TREATMENT

Treatment options in Arizona range from residential, 12-step approaches to maintenance doses of methadone and counseling at outpatient clinics. There's a huge disparity in the costs of these programs.

One Phoenix-based nonprofit sober living home, 5A, charges residents a little more than $400 per month, including meals, and asks residents to commit to staying for three months.

A month of treatment at an in-patient center that incorporates the sometimes-controversial medicines methadone or buprenorphine into their treatment plans could cost an addict – or, in some cases, an addict's family – more than 30 times as much.

Thirty days of inpatient treatment at the nonprofit center Valley Hope of Chandler costs $15,500 – more than $500 per day. Treatment centers that market themselves as "luxury," with features such as equine therapy and rock climbing, could cost $40,000 to $50,000 for a 30-day program.

Susan Romeo said it cost $40,000 for her son Joey to receive three weeks of treatment at Sierra Tucson, a rehab center known for treating several celebrities. He left the program before his 30-day treatment program ended.

Some inpatient treatment for opioid addicts can run as high as $80,000 per month, Geren said.

"I don't think any kind of care matches $80,000 a month," she said. "You're talking about a year's salary."

Geren said she knows families who have spent between $50,000 and $100,000 – their life savings.

Outpatient treatment is available, usually at a much lesser cost. A year of outpatient methadone treatment, for example, costs about $4,700.

This type of treatment is also much cheaper than putting an addict in prison or jail. A year in jail can cost about five times more than a year of methadone treatment, according to the National Institute of Drug Abuse.

Romeo's family pared back on their spending to pay for the care he needed.

"Everything I have is from the thrift shop," Susan said.

She lives with her husband in a one-story house they bought as a foreclosure on the outskirts of Tucson. It has a pool in the backyard and mountain views.

"People look at our house, and go, 'Oh wow, they must have money.' Well, no, you don't know my story," Susan said. "You don't know that when we had to coat the roof, I coated the roof. We didn't call someone to coat the roof."

RANGE OF TREATMENT OPTIONS

The World Health Organization says detox alone – which basically means medical supervision while an addict goes through withdrawal – commonly leads to relapse and is rarely enough to help someone recover from opioid dependence. It recommends a diverse array of treatment options because no single form of treatment works for all people.

On one side of the spectrum, there are opioid treatment centers, which provide inpatient and outpatient treatment and incorporate methadone and/or buprenorphine.

These drugs imitate how opiates act within the brain, latching on to receptors that create a sense of euphoria. However, methadone and buprenorphine don't fit into those receptors as well as opiates do – meaning that the right dose can eliminate withdrawal symptoms without causing the patient to feel high.

Still, these pharmaceuticals have appeared on the street and in prisons.

Nick Stavros, CEO of Scottsdale-based Community Medical Services, said their clinics take precautions to prevent methadone from becoming abused, including requiring patients to drink methadone in front of a nurse for a certain period of time before they can go home with doses.

At the Phoenix clinic, nurses keep bottles of methadone locked in a safe behind the counter. The clinic normally treats 300 to 400 people each day.

Some states have pushed back against expanded access to medication-assisted treatment. West Virginia, for example, has a moratorium on the opening of new opioid treatment centers in the state.

Stavros said banning medication-assisted treatment "is dissuading people from getting the one treatment that could save their lives. It's totally terrible."

Treatment facilities that dispense these medications must follow rigorous guidelines, including obtaining certification from the Drug Enforcement Administration and the federal government. Arizona has 36 such accredited opioid treatment programs, according to the Substance Abuse and Mental Health Services Administration.

Facilities that don't provide these medications must still obtain a state license if they plan to provide medical care.

On the other side of the spectrum are sober living homes, which provide a post-detox, medication-free environment.

Arizona doesn't track the number of sober living homes in the state, but some estimates reach as high as 10,000, according to a story by KPHO in Phoenix. Scottsdale officials believe more than 100 sober living homes operate within the city.

These homes take a 12-step approach.

In the 40,000-person city of Prescott, the sober living home industry exploded, causing resentment among local residents. Rep. Noel Campbell, R-Prescott, said he knew about 173 sober living homes operating without any regulations when he started working on legislation. He introduced a bill to raise the standard of care at these homes, and the governor signed the bill into law in May 2016.

"It was a horror story," he said.

LACK OF RESOURCES

Six years ago, Joanne Buchan, the mother of a recovering addict, said she couldn't find a treatment center in Arizona that would accept her son's Blue Cross Blue Shield insurance without a $5,000 copay. She said she managed to find one in California.

"We didn't know where to turn or what to do," she said. "There are people who say they will help you, but we found out they were like brokers. They would get commission for sending you to certain places."

The Governor's Office of Youth, Faith and Family has a treatment locator where users can filter facilities by location, type and forms of payment accepted.

"It's a great first step," said Samuel Burba, a program administrator with the office. "Finding and locating treatment – unfortunately – is a maze and people don't know where to start."

This locator is a great asset, Geren said, but is not comprehensive, and families still need to do their own research about the quality of care provided by each facility.

Researchers at Arizona State University also have pieced together a list of treatment programs.

The guide identifies nearly 100 opioid treatment programs in the state as of August 2015 and lists the type of treatment provided by each center (alcohol and/or opioid abuse) and the forms of payment each one accepts. Some do not take any form of insurance.

Adrienne Lindsey, a researcher at ASU who worked on the guide, said the team compiled information from state and national lists of providers and did their own research. Many providers don't appear on any registries, so the team often found them by searching the internet.

Even when somebody does find a treatment center, they might not be able to get in right away. Those involved in the industry locally said addicts enrolled in the Arizona Health Care Cost Containment System, the state's Medicaid program, often face waiting lists for treatment programs. Officials with AHCCCS have not provided a response.

Susan Romeo recommends that people carefully vet each center. Some can earn a reputation for having less-than-average, or even dangerous, standards of care.

"Every rehab center has a beautiful website. When you call them, they tell you exactly what you want to hear," Romeo said. "Question everything, get things in writing. If you have a child in treatment, show up at that treatment center. Take a look at that treatment center. There are certain red flags. If you call and you're not getting anyone on the phone, no good. Any reputable place is gonna have a full-time receptionist."

Six years after he first got hooked, Joey Romeo now shares an apartment in a sober living home on the outskirts of Mesa with another recovering addict.

He moved in shortly after completing a 60-day inpatient program.

The sober living home, run by SOBA, costs about $150 per week. He said many of the staff are recovering addicts who have been clean for years.

Romeo said it would be easy for him to find drugs no matter where he is, even at the closest bus stop.

"I'll be out there during the day, I'm gonna run into s---," Romeo said. "That's just how it works. I can get through that stuff and come back here and talk to someone. I have a place to come back to, a safe space."

1. According to this article, what are the most effective forms of treatment for opioid addiction?

2. What do you think about the treatment industry that has popped up during the opioid epidemic? Do you think it is based on making money? Or does it really help people get clean?

CHAPTER 5

WHAT THE MEDIA SAY

Newspaper editors are noticing that deaths among opioid users, as reported in their papers, are closely connected to other health care statistics. An editorial in the *New York Times* in 2016 stated that in Texas, "according to a study in the journal *Obstetrics & Gynecology*, the maternal mortality rate doubled from 17.7 per 100,000 live births in 2000 to 35.8 in 2014. Compare that with Germany, which had 4.1 deaths per 100,000 live births in 2014." According to reports from a task force created by the Texas Legislature, the biggest killers during and after pregnancy in Texas are cardiac problems and prescription opioid or illegal drug overdoses.

The *Times* editors went on to suggest that Texas lawmakers could approach solutions to some of these problems "by investing more in health clinics in minority communities and in mental health and addiction treatment." They also believe another very helpful tactic would be expanding Medicare so that more low-income Americans would be covered. However, they noted the responses they recommend to the opioid epidemic have not been happening in Texas and in several other states: "Texas is one of 19 states that have refused to expand Medicaid under the Affordable Care Act, despite the law's generous terms, with the federal government picking up nearly all of the cost for low-income families."[1]

"HOW THE NATION'S OPIOID EPIDEMIC IS MORPHING – AND GROWING," BY CHARLES ORNSTEIN, FROM *PROPUBLICA*, OCTOBER 3, 2016

The nation's opioid epidemic shows no signs of abating—and in fact may be headed in a far more dangerous direction.

That's the conclusion of journalist David Armstrong, who has been chronicling the scourge this year for STAT, a new health and medicine website. Armstrong has written about how heroin and, increasingly, fentanyl have overtaken narcotic painkillers as the drugs of choice for addicts — presenting new challenges for law enforcement and health professionals.

In the past few months, Armstrong has told the story of two best friends in Ohio who became addicted to heroin and what happened when one of them died in 2015 after taking drugs supplied by the other. He's also written about an eerie photo released by an Ohio police department showing a little boy strapped into his car seat while two adults in the front seat are passed out from overdoses.

Armstrong's news organization, STAT, has also gone back in time to understand the roots of the epidemic. It filed motions to unseal court records from the 1990s and 2000s to learn more about how drug companies marketed their painkillers and got Americans hooked. The news organization won a motion in Kentucky to unseal court records, a decision that's under appeal by Purdue Pharma, the maker of OxyContin. STAT had more success in West Virginia, where it obtained records showing how Abbott Laboratories helped Purdue market OxyContin to doctors — including giving one doctor a box full of donuts shaped to spell out "OxyContin."

We talked to Armstrong last week. Highlights are below, edited for length and clarity.

It's not a surprise to anybody in this country that we're facing an epidemic of opioid overdoses and that the problem seems to be getting worse over time. What makes you as a reporter interested in covering a story that perhaps some people feel that they already know?

The reason we thought it was important to cover the opioid crisis is really twofold. One, as you mentioned, STAT is a new publication and we're focused on medicine, health and science, and to my way of thinking, in terms of a public health issue, at this moment in this country, there's nothing more pressing than the opioid crisis. So, from that standpoint, I felt it was important that we cover this and sort of put our stake in the ground.

The other thing that really troubled me about this and piqued my interest in doing more was the rise of fentanyl. You know, fentanyl is so potent and is really adding to the death toll in a way that we haven't seen, and I wanted to know more about that. I wanted to know what was going on, and part of that is learning more about how we got here in addition to what's going on now.

Is the emergence of fentanyl related to efforts to crack down on prescription painkillers?

That's part of it. In areas where we've seen restrictions on prescribers and very aggressive prescription monitoring programs, there's no question that some people who are abusing opioid painkillers or prescription painkillers transition to heroin. But drug dealers and cartels are pretty smart, pretty cynical, and what they saw was a rise in the use of opioids and they realized that they could initially produce heroin cheaper and supply that sort of same population with a similar high, similar drug at a lower cost. So those two things sort of happened in parallel tracks, even though we did have people switching from one to the other. And now with fentanyl, we're just seeing more of the same, except it's just more profitable for drug dealers.

You wrote a piece that was really compelling about two best friends, from Ohio actually, teenagers DJ Shanks and Justin Laycock, and their relationship and their bonding over drugs, and I found it really compelling. How did you get turned on to this story and why did you decide that this was a story that needed to be written?

DJ and Justin, best friends since kindergarten, grew up to have an addiction problem together, but they were heroin users, and it also started with prescription painkillers. They were using Vicodin. They accidentally used heroin laced with fentanyl. Justin brought the drug to DJ who was working at a Tim Horton's doughnut shop at the time, and he snorted it and he died on the job. One of the more compelling aspects of that story is what happened to Justin. He wasn't his drug dealer. He was helping out a friend, he thought, because DJ told him he was "dope sick" and needed something. So Justin brought it to him, didn't charge him. He paid for it, and he was arrested. He was charged with a crime, a drug charge crime, but that carried a mandatory prison sentence. The thing that really caught me on this story was that to get help, Justin had to plead guilty to a higher charge of manslaughter, because that would allow the judge to put him in a treatment program as part of his probation after his prison sentence, and he wants to get sober. He hates being an addict. I thought that was really kind of an indictment of where we are in terms of treatment in this country.

What is the wrongdoing here? Who is falling down on the job here and what needs to be fixed as far as the problem that is repeating itself across the country?

For starters, we've done, as a country and the U.S. government, a poor job of eliminating the source of the drugs, which is primarily China. Now some of that's out of our control, of course, but it hasn't been as much of a priority as it should be. In fairness, you know the problem is so difficult to solve because we have multiple laboratories in China and some other countries in Asia that are sending this product to criminal syndicates in Canada, to Mexican cartels. So then there's numerous people with laboratories that can translate this drug into pill form or put it into heroin, and it's so multifaceted. There's so many organizations doing it that it's almost like whack-a-mole.

In 2007, we had a similar outbreak of fentanyl overdoses. Well it was one lab in Mexico that was producing it and the DEA and the Mexican government uncovered it, they shut the lab down, the problem went away. That's not going to happen this time.

1. How can journalists be useful when they report on the opioid epidemic? Who will their stories benefit?

"MAKER OF DEADLY FENTANYL KICKS IN HALF A MILLION TO DEFEAT POT LEGALIZATION IN ARIZONA: BIG PHARMA HAS LONG BEEN ACCUSED OF TRYING TO BLOCK MARIJUANA LEGALIZATION," BY PHILLIP SMITH, FROM *ALTERNET*, SEPTEMBER 9, 2016

Marijuana legalization advocates have long argued that pharmaceutical companies, which could lose out if marijuana is legally available, are some of the staunchest supporters of pot prohibition, and now an Arizona company is making their case for them.

According to campaign finance reports posted online by the Arizona secretary of state's office, fentanyl manufacturer Insys Therapuetics has donated $500,000 to foes of the Prop 205 marijuana legalization initiative.

Fentanyl is a synthetic opioid several dozen times more potent than heroin. It has been linked to numerous opioid overdose deaths across the country, especially when mixed with heroin. Marijuana, on the other hand, has no reported overdose deaths, ever.

Insys isn't just any pharmaceutical company. Its sole product is Subsys, a sublingual fentanyl spray, and the company has shown that it's willing to bend the rules to sell that product. In the past month alone, two former company employees pleaded not guilty to federal charges related to an alleged kickback scheme to get doctors to prescribe Subsys, and Illinois Attorney General Lisa Madigan filed a lawsuit against the company charging that Insys hawked the drug to doctors for off-label prescribing.

Insys' "desire for increased profits led it to disregard

patients' health and push addictive opioids for non-FDA approved purposes," Madigan wrote.

While Subsys is the only product the company currently markets, it says on its website that it is also working "to develop pharmaceutical cannabinoids." It's not much of a leap to wonder whether the company is backing the continued criminalization of marijuana users in order to protect potential market share for its products in development, and legalization supporters were quick to do so.

Responding to a query from *US News & World Report*, the anti-legalization group Arizonans for Responsible Drug Policy said it would not return the donation. Instead, it released a statement expressing gratitude for the donation and pointing out that Insys is an Arizona-based company, unlike the Marijuana Policy Project (MPP), which backs the legalization effort.

The MPP-backed Arizona Campaign to Regulate Marijuana Like Alcohol responded with a statement from campaign director J.P. Holyoak, who laid into both Insys and the opposition group that took its money. He said:

> We are truly shocked by our opponents' decision to keep a donation from what appears to be one of the more unscrupulous members of Big Pharma. You have a company using profits from the sale of what has been called 'the most potent and dangerous opioid on the market' to prevent adults from using a far less harmful substance. In addition to selling an extremely potent and dangerous opioid, they have been under investigation by numerous states and the federal government for the manner in which they have done so.

"Their homepage touts their development of 'pharmaceutical cannabinoids,' which are synthetic versions of chemical compounds found in marijuana," he continued. "It appears they are trying to kill a non-pharmaceutical market for marijuana in order to line their own pockets."

"Our opponents have made a conscious decision to associate with this company. They are now funding their campaign with profits from the sale of opioids—and maybe even the improper sale of opioids. We hope that every Arizonan understands that Arizonans for Responsible Drug Policy is now a complete misnomer. Their entire campaign is tainted by this money. Any time an ad airs against Prop. 205, the voters should know that it was paid for by highly suspect Big Pharma actors," he concluded.

1. What could motivate a political campaign to accept donations from a maker of opioids?

2. What could motivate a pharmaceutical company to fund drug policy campaigns?

COMMENT ON "WHAT'S THE WORST THING YOU'VE SEEN," BY BRAYDEN CLUFF, POSTED ON *REDDIT*

Well, these clinics are meant to help the under served. So it's not like we're getting the normal cross section of society.

Typically (I'm an EMT but I'm working on a medical school application) I work in the medical area and the people that we see are generally at least 50 lbs. overweight, don't practice the best hygiene, and want a pill to solve their back pain. 90% of the people that I work with would have all of their health problems amelio-rated with a change in diet and an increase in exercise.

This is my dilemma as a healthcare provider. The reason that I got into this field is because I care about people and I wanted to do more for the human race than sit in an office and try to make money. But many times day in and day out, the people that you are dealing with are abrasive, ungrateful, noncompliant with treatment plans or advice, and mad that you won't give them morphine or a refillable prescription for percocet or hydrocodone.

90% of the time, you're not dealing with the cream of the crop as far as the human race goes. It is an easy trap to fall into though to become cynical about that and look down on these people.

I can't really explain the mindset that you have to be in. But you have to be able to show compassion, and give care to everyone who enters your care. I have to remind myself that I don't know the circumstances of these people's lives and that I may have done far worse if I'd only been given what they had.

1. Would personal knowledge of pain help healthcare providers to better understand the needs of opioid users seeking their help?

2. How might healthcare providers respond to opioid-addicted patients in different ways due to their experiences in the field?

"BIG PHARMA'S "STRANGLEHOLD" ON CONGRESS WORSENING OPIOID EPIDEMIC: FORMER DEA OFFICIAL TELLS THE GUARDIAN HOW HUNDREDS OF MILLIONS ARE BEING SPENT TO PROTECT PHARMACEUTICAL INDUSTRY," BY LAUREN MCCAULEY, FROM *COMMON DREAMS*, OCTOBER 31, 2016

If it seems like Big Pharma has escaped accountability for its role in perpetuating the nation's deadly opioid epidemic, those suspicions are not unfounded.

According to a former top Drug Enforcement Administration (DEA) official, the industry's influence over Congress has successfully quashed efforts to regulate the pharmaceutical drug market aiding an unprecedented addiction to legal drugs.

"When you sit with a parent who can't understand why there's so many pharmaceuticals out in the illicit marketplace, and why isn't the government doing anything, well the DEA was doing something. Unfortunately what we're trying to do is thwarted by people who are writing laws," Joseph Rannazzisi, who for 10 years served as head of the DEA's Diversion Control Division, told the *Guardian*.

In an exclusive investigation published on Monday, the *Guardian*, with Rannazzisi's help, explains how Congress turned its back on suffering families and, under the guise of combating the national epidemic, has routinely passed legislation that effectively shields the industry.

One such law is the recently-passed Ensuring Patient Access and Effective Drug Enforcement Act, which "requires the DEA to warn pharmacies and distributors if they are in breach of regulations"—namely "crooked doctors and pharmacists" in suspicion of over-prescribing prescription drugs—"and to give them a chance to comply before licenses are withdrawn," the *Guardian* reports.

Rannazzisi declared the new law a "gift to the industry," explaining how it does neither of the things it purports to do. "This doesn't ensure patient access and it doesn't help drug enforcement at all," he said. "What this bill does is take away DEA's ability to go after a pharma-cist, a wholesaler, manufacturer or distributor."

"The bill passed because 'Big Pharma' wanted it to pass," he added. "When I was in charge what I tried to do was explain to my investigators and my agents that our job was to regulate the industry and they're not going to like being regulated."

The *Washington Post* has also been reporting on the drop in enforcement actions against pharmaceutical distrib-utors, dubbed "pill mills," which it said was due in part to "resistance from higher-level Justice Department officials who were being heavily lobbied by the wholesalers."

Indeed, as the *Guardian* points out, the industry "has spent hundreds of millions of dollars in lobbying to stave off measures to reduce prescriptions and therefore sales of opioid painkillers."

The Guardian continues:

> Among the most influential drug industry groups is the Pain Care Forum, co-founded by a top execu-tive of Purdue Pharma – the manufacturer of the opioid which unleashed the addiction epidemic, OxyContin—and largely funded by pharmaceutical companies. It spent $740m lobbying Congress and

state legislatures over the past decade according to the Center for Public Integrity.

Recipients of political donations from the industry included Senator Orrin Hatch, chairman of the finance committee, who took $360,000 and Representative Mike Rogers, who received more than $300,000, according to the CPI.

Both Hatch and Rogers were reportedly "instrumental in legislation establishing a panel to examine treatment of pain that critics said had close ties to industry-funded groups."

The problem of industry-influenced "pain management" panels was also highlighted earlier this year by *Intercept* reporter Lee Fang, who uncovered Big Pharma's attempt to influence recently reissued guidelines from Centers for Disease Control (CDC) on opioid prescriptions.

One lawmaker who has been a vocal critical of this industry collusion is Sen. Ron Wyden (D-Ore.), who said, "There is no question that the powerful opioid manufacturers have a disproportionate voice, a disproportionate amount of influence, in these debates."

"Congress would rather listen to people who had a profit motive rather than a public health and safety motive," said Rannazzisi. "As long as the industry has this stranglehold through lobbyists, nothing's going to change."

According to (pdf) [*Editor's note: Links can be found with the original article.*] the U.S. Department of Health and Human Services, "[s]ince 1999, the rate of overdose deaths involving opioids—including prescription opioid pain relievers and heroin—nearly quadrupled," as over 165,000 people have died from prescription opioid overdoses.

1. How can people depend on their elected representatives to improve legislation about opioid use if there are pharmaceutical corporations influencing the elected officials?

"AN UNINTENDED SIDE EFFECT OF TRANSPARENCY," BY STEPHEN ENGELBERG, FROM *PROPUBLICA*, MAY 12, 2016

In 2013, ProPublica released Prescriber Checkup, a database that detailed the prescribing habits of hundreds of thousands of doctors across the country.

ProPublica reporters used the data—which reflected prescriptions covered by Medicare's massive drug program, known as part D — to uncover several important findings. The data showed doctors often prescribed narcotic painkillers and antipsychotic drugs in quantities that could be dangerous for their patients, many of whom were elderly. The reporters also found evidence that some doctors wrote far, far more prescriptions than their peers for expensive brand-name drugs for which there were cheaper generic alternatives. And we found instances of probable fraud that had gone undetected by the government.

The data proved equally useful for others: Doctors themselves turned to Prescriber Checkup to assess how they compared to their peers. Medical plan administrators and hospitals checked it to see whether their doctors were following best practices in treating patients. Law enforcement officials searched the database for leads on fraud and illicit trafficking in pain medications. Patients turned to the data to vet their doctors' drug choices and compare them with others in their specialties.

Recently, though, we picked up clear signs that some readers are using the data for another purpose: To search for doctors likely to prescribe them some widely abused drugs, many of them opioids.

Like nearly everyone on the web, we use Google Analytics to collect data on our site. So far this year, it appears that perhaps as many as 25 percent of Prescriber Checkup's page views involve narcotic painkillers, anti-anxiety medications, and amphetamines.

Thousands of the people visiting those pages initially viewed the "reporting recipe" we wrote to help local journalists identify doctors who ranked among the top prescribers of narcotics. The readership for this recipe far exceeds any reasonable estimate of local or regional journalists researching stories. According to our web data, many readers also arrived at Prescriber Checkup after web searches like "doctors who prescribe narcotics easily" or "doctors that will prescribe anything."

It's not possible to draw definitive conclusions about the motives of these people. Some, no doubt, legitimately have chronic pain or anxiety and are simply looking for doctors who will help them. Two of the more frequently searched drugs are Suboxone and methadone, medicines used to treat opioid addiction. (As the depth of the opiod epidemic has become clear, some doctors have become reluctant to prescribe these drugs out of fears that they, too, can be abused.) Still, it seems probable that some of the readers who visit Prescriber Checkup are looking for doctors who will prescribe narcotics and other powerful stimulants with few or no questions asked.

This is not a new problem for journalists, or others whose business is providing or sharing information. In another era, burglars would read the obituary pages so they could target the homes of people who had just died. More recently, terrorists have used search engines to find recipes for bomb-making or encrypted communications. Con artists have found new ways to perpetrate schemes through Facebook and other social media.

The Internet's leading platforms have struggled with this issue. Just this week, Google announced that it would not accept ads for payday lenders. Both Facebook and Google bar advertising for guns, explosives and recreational drugs.

We impose comparable limits on the advertising we are willing to accept on our site. But as a news organization dedicated to pursuing stories with "moral force," we feel we also have an obligation to look hard at possible misuses of our journalism.

We have long been advocates for transparency and have repeatedly pushed government agencies to release more data on everything from dialysis clinics to complications in surgical procedures performed under Medicare. In almost every one of these instances, some government officials argued against making the information public, warning that the information would be misused.

Initially, when we published Prescriber Checkup, we had to request the data under the Freedom of Information Act. The government has come around to see the value of releasing prescribing information. Now, the Centers for Medicare and Medicaid Services puts the data freely on its own site. It even has a tool that allows people to compare doctors based on their opioid prescribing, just as our site does.

We continue to believe that Prescriber Checkup provides significant and beneficial insights into prescribing patterns — insights that can help patients, practitioners, regulators and a variety of other users. Doctors, the vast majority of whom want to do the right thing, have told us that this is the only place where they can measure their prescribing against colleagues in their specialty and state. And we regularly hear from law enforcement and medical board regulators across the country who say our tool helped them focus their efforts in ways that previously were not available.

Still, we recognize that it's important not to ignore the not-so-beneficial uses of Prescriber Checkup. As one way of doing this, we are adding a warning to the pages of all narcotic drugs that reminds readers of the serious health risks posed by taking opioids for pain relief. We will also link to advice on their use by the Centers for Disease Control and Prevention and have written a story on the growing public health crisis arising from the abuse prescription pain medication. We will continue to report on this issue, as we've done previously.

Data journalism gives readers access to a stunning array of information on everything from healthcare to election results. As data sets grow ever larger, they also introduce ethical questions that journalists will be weighing for many years to come. We hope the actions we've taken contribute to that conversation.

1. What responsibilities do journalists have when it comes to reporting on the opioid epidemic?

2. Do you think the media should be less transparent if this prevents those who are addicted to opioids from getting information that could possibly harm them?

"ARIZONA MEDICAL BOARDS CAN TAKE YEARS TO PENALIZE DOCTORS WHO OVERPRESCRIBE," BY AGNEL PHILIP AND EMILY L. MAHONEY, FROM *CRONKITE NEWS*, JANUARY 5, 2017

PHOENIX — One patient, a 29-year-old woman, was prescribed a dangerous cocktail of anti-anxiety drugs and opioids by her Fort Mohave doctor after a car accident. Another, this time a 61-year-old man with back pain, was given a potentially fatal dose of painkillers, including fentanyl, an opiate 30 to 50 times stronger than heroin.

Nearly five years after his first documented instance of overprescribing, the doctor's medical license was suspended in August by the Arizona Medical Board. Three months later in November, authorities arrested him in Wyoming for allegedly prescribing an illegal amount of opioids to residents of five states, according to a complaint filed with the Wyoming's U.S. District Attorney's Office.

In Yuma, a doctor was forced to surrender his license last year after prescribing large quantities of controlled substances, including narcotic pain and anti-anxiety medications to a patient who died of drug and alcohol toxicity. The prescribing "continued until her death," records show.

Although the number of doctors and physician assistants sanctioned for overprescribing opiates — just 250 during the past 16 years — is small compared to the more than 19,000 currently licensed to prescribe controlled substances, the boards' disciplinary records detail more than 1,000 instances of overprescribing, sometimes after the doctor received multiple reprimands. In the most egregious cases, doctors prescribe opiates like OxyContin, Vicodin, Percocet, Dilaudid and others en masse for profit, often without performing any medical exams.

It can take years for a physician to be penalized and revocations are rare, according to a Cronkite News examination of hundreds of disciplinary records from the Arizona Medical Board, Arizona Board of Physician Assistants and the Arizona Board of Osteopathic Examiners. In the meantime, many of these physicians continue to practice.

"What I'd say to doctors is make sure that you understand the facts on these incredible products and make sure that they're getting to the people that need them, that we're avoiding it if someone has already beat addiction, or is an alcoholic and is a substance abuser, that we're asking the right questions," Arizona Gov. Doug Ducey said.

"And to the doctors who are abusing these products and are a part of these drug dealers that are trying to use the law or a regulation, that are trying to run cover for them, not only are we going to fix that, but we are going to find you as well."

Cronkite News conducted a four-month investigation into the rise of prescription opioid abuse in Arizona. Dozens of journalists at Arizona State University examined thousands of records and traveled across the state to interview addicts, law enforcement, public officials and health care experts. The goal: uncover the root of the epidemic, explain the ramifications and provide solutions.

Since 2010, more than 3,600 people have overdosed and died from opioids in Arizona. In 2015, the dead numbered 701 – the highest of any year before, or nearly two per day, according to an analysis by the Arizona Department of Health Services.

Experts say the opioid epidemic is not limited to doctors who intentionally overprescribe potent painkillers.

Just last year, U.S. Surgeon General Vivek H. Murthy issued a national report calling for a "cultural shift in how we think about addiction," urging doctors and health care providers to be more diligent when prescribing dangerous drugs even to patients who may need them.

"A recent study found that doctors continue to prescribe opioids for 91 percent of patients who suffered a non-fatal overdose, with 63 percent of those patients continuing to receive high doses; 17 percent of these patients overdosed again within two years," the report found.

Arizona has remained among the top states for the amount of oxycodone and morphine its pharmacies, hospitals and doctors have purchased per person since the Drug Enforcement Administration began publishing data in 2000. In 2015, more than 2 million grams of oxycodone alone came into the state, the third-highest total per capita in the country.

The state boards that regulate and license doctors in Arizona rely almost entirely on complaints from concerned residents or patients' families members. Patricia McSorley, executive director of the Arizona Medical Board and Arizona Board of Physician Assistants – which regulate most medical doctors and all physician assistants in the state – declined to be interviewed for this story.

Jenna Jones, executive director of the Arizona Board of Osteopathic Examiners, which regulates the state's 3,200 doctors of osteopathy, said the board is trying to help its doctors detect potential addicts before prescribing drugs.

"The opioid prescribing problem is not limited to one area," she said. "It's just something that's hard to get your hands on. We're trying to give doctors ideas of how to recognize drug-seeking behavior and how to deal with that."

Dr. Shakeel Kahn, the Fort Mohave doctor arrested in November, spent years openly disputing his prescribing methods with local pharmacies while he continued to dole out pills with little action from the Arizona Medical Board. He sent letters to pharmacies in 2012 demanding that they fill his prescriptions for powerful opiate painkillers or prepare for a lawsuit.

Kahn made good on his promise, suing two pharmacies and pharmacists, one of whom called Kahn a "quack" who was "contributing to drug abuse in the Bullhead City area," according to court documents.

He lost both lawsuits.

At the time, the medical board sent Kahn a "non-disciplinary" advisory letter, saying his record keeping was questionable for several patients who were prescribed several opioids. Until recently, his only formal sanction was in 2010 for an alleged patient abandonment case in which he increased doses of Dilaudid, an opioid, even though she was already "lethargic and sleepy," possibly causing her to develop "pneumonia with acute respiratory failure while hospitalized," records show.

At the height of their treatment with Kahn, two of his patients were taking the equivalent of 3,032 and 1,820 milligrams of morphine per day. A report by the Centers for Disease Control and Prevention discouraged doctors from prescribing more than 90 milligrams daily because of a high risk of a fatal overdose.

Kahn's clinic, located in a strip mall across State Route 95 from Valley View Medical Center in Fort Mohave, had no markings but for a piece of paper taped to the inside of the door displaying operating hours, a phone number to call for appointments and a warning that he did not accept walk-ins. His attorney Thomas Price refused to comment, citing "ongoing legal proceedings."

The Arizona State Board of Pharmacy maintains a database of doctors, patients and prescriptions called the Controlled Substances Prescription Monitoring Program, which can aid in physician disciplinary investigations. But state law prevents the boards from using it without an open investigation.

The DEA also has a database that can track prescription drugs from manufacturer to patient, but it isn't typically used as a source of tips for criminal investigations because of the volume of drugs that it tracks, said Doug Coleman, the DEA special agent in charge of the Phoenix division, which oversees controlled substance registrations for tens of thousands of health professionals in Arizona.

"Unless someone gives us a tip, the chance of us finding (a doctor who is mishandling medication) from a regular regulatory inspection are remote," Coleman said. "There are just so many more of them than there are of us, so it make take three to four years before we figure it out."

Sometimes overprescribing doctors, like Tucson's Robert C. Osborne, are criminally charged. He was indicted in December 2014 after allegedly prescribing hundreds of milligrams of opioids to his patients and fraudulently billing Medicare for pills his patients didn't need. He has pleaded not guilty.

One of these patients was a 52-year-old Tucson nurse who had been an addict for years. Her dosages kept increasing under Osborne — even when she failed drug tests, records show. She was found dead in 2010, with four different medications in her blood.

"She was prescribed fentanyl patches, and those were the ones that she abused. Instead of putting them on her skin, she would chew them," said the woman's daughter, Jamie Dutton, 38. "I was lectured by all the pharmacists and all the pharmacy technicians. I was told when I picked her medications up or when I dropped off the prescriptions, they felt that she was being overprescribed and it was reported to the DEA."

Osborne's case is pending.

Deaths by opioid overdoses in Arizona, which include heroin, have increased from about 620 in 2014 to 701 in 2015, according to the Arizona Department of Health Services. Thousands of drug users required emergency room care after an overdose.

So-called "pill mills," where doctors like Osborne allegedly exchanged cash for pills, are investigated by law enforcement just as they would investigate an illegal drug ring. Those, too, take time.

"In Arizona, there are millions and millions of pills that make their way into our communities. Many of these pills are highly addictive," said Stephen Duplissis, section chief for the Health Care Fraud and Abuse section of the Arizona Attorney General's Office. "So we have to think about, how did these pills, these highly addictive pills, make their way into Arizona communities? Well, one way they make their way into Arizona communities is when we have a doctor that's willing to prescribe drugs for no legitimate medical purpose, but simply for profit."

"What we have is a society that is functioning day in and day out, and they're high," Duplissis said.

The Arizona Medical Board had prohibited Alaaeldin Babiker, the Yuma doctor who surrendered his license in April after his patient died, from prescribing controlled substances two years earlier. He was disciplined for opioid dependence, among other addictions, and for prescribing drugs to his wife.

When board officials went to his office, patients filled the waiting room and he was nowhere to be found. There were "used syringes, needles, dirty cotton balls and other unsanitary materials strewn on the floor and on desks," disciplinary records show.

Unlike Babiker, some overprescribing doctors are disciplined multiple times without lasting restrictions on their license.

One physician in Casa Grande, Michael Ridge, prescribed a mixture of Vicodin and other drugs for years to a 20-year-old patient, who the doctor noted was "craving opioids," records show. The man made three suicide attempts while in the doctor's care, one of which was reported by his mother.

About a year after the man's first appointment, Ridge "received notice from a pharmacy that (the man) was receiving controlled substances from other providers." After briefly cutting him off, Ridge continued his prescriptions.

The Arizona Medical Board reprimanded Ridge without restrictions, finding that he "prescribed narcotics for chronic pain without performing an evaluation of the pain problem." He was later put on probation for similar offenses. Ridge did not respond to requests for comment. He still is practicing.

1. Why are doctors not often penalized for overprescribing opioids?

2. Would disciplinary action against doctors who overprescribe opioids, in your opinion, help in the fight against the opioid epidemic? Why or why not?

CHAPTER 6

WHAT ORDINARY PEOPLE SAY

I t's hard for some opioid users to express themselves clearly. "It was as if we were interviewing zombies; the speech and movements of those we met were so bogged down by opiates that they were often hard to understand," states author Chris Hedges. When he interviewed people for a book on poor populations in the United States who, in many cases, suffer disproportionately from drug addictions, he "found not only decayed and impoverished communities but shattered lives." One of the men he met said that over the last few years he had seen a lot of arrests in the county, adding, "A lot of the people that have been arrested are elderly people that are sellin' their medication just to live."[1]

Some advocates for legalizing street drugs admit that punishing these people through prison sentences won't help anyone. "For some addicts, it wouldn't—they'd be no better off, but no worse off either," said Conor Friedersdorf in an article for *The Atlantic*. He believes that "legalization would mean less likelihood of death by overdose due to standardization of supply and dosage." Also, people would be able to seek medical attention for themselves or family members without fear of being arrested.

Parents who have lost children to opioid use have also been learning to put aside their family's shame and speak their minds. "Some of these mothers blame clinicians for prescribing highly-addictive drugs to their sons and daughters," writes author C. J. Arlotta in the preface for a book on these family losses. She observes that "others fault federal agencies for not doing enough to protect our country's citizenry; and the majority of them accuse overpowering pharmaceutical companies for misleading practitioners through false advertising."[3] In such a complex epidemic, the blame for such levels of opioid addiction can certainly be passed around, from politicians, to Big Pharma, to doctors, and, of course, to the addicts themselves. But blame is not always useful for finding needed solutions to these problems; rather, it might be helpful to have compassion for the addicts themselves.

"THE NEED FOR COMPASSION: DR. ALANA HIRSH REFLECTS ON HER JOURNEY INTO ADDICTION MEDICINE, AND WHY SELF-LOVE CAN GO A LONG WAY TOWARD HELPING OTHERS," BY ALANA HIRSH, FROM *THE GLOBE AND MAIL*, SEPTEMBER 1, 2016

In the discussion about Canadian drug policy, the unspoken question is: why should we take care of drug addicts? I have had to ask myself this because my job is taking care of people with drug dependence and mental illness in the Downtown Eastside, Vancouver's notoriously drug and disease-ridden inner city. What does society gain from assisting people who engage in illegal activity, who bring their diseases, and, with increasing prevalence, their death, upon themselves?

I am a McGill and UBC-trained family and emergency physician, and have practised in Canada, the United States, and West Africa. I have delivered babies, treated trauma victims, managed chronic disease, and comforted dying people. And, the truth is, in spite of having had my prescriptions forged, my car broken into, having been threatened and lied to, I enjoy, and feel privileged to treat people afflicted by drug dependence. Drug addicts are my favourite patients.

I stumbled into addiction medicine during a period of disillusionment in my medical education. I was leaning toward specializing in plastic surgery, and had arranged to do my family medicine rotation in Vancouver, mostly for the chance to explore the West Coast. I discovered on my arrival that the doctor I was shadowing worked mainly with pregnant heroin addicts. Sometimes he just sat me in a room with them: "Ask her to tell you her story," he instructed.

Josie was 16 and pregnant. She had long brown hair and a childish, angelic face. She came from Winnipeg, where there was a warrant out for her arrest. The only person she knew in B.C. was her boyfriend, the father of her child. She was on a methadone program, but was giving half of her dose to her boyfriend to keep him off heroin (he was unable to get a doctor). As a result, by midnight every night she would experience terrible withdrawal symptoms. Withdrawal has been described to me by addicts as "feeling like you are going to die," and the physiologic effects of it actually did put her fetus at risk of death. So she would sell her body to get money for drugs. She had no family to turn to – her mother had been shooting her up with heroin since she was a baby. She was so skinny – only 106 pounds in her seventh month – and so desperate. "Man, don't ever do heroin," she advised me with a rueful smile. She was a good person, a child, trapped in a horribly addicted body.

Since then, I have listened to hundreds of stories. Debra, born to parents who were addicts themselves, had a father who sold her to his friends for extra cash. Jeff's mother died when he was nine months old, and his father was an alcoholic who beat him. Ryan's mother tried to commit suicide four times before he turned 10, once by putting her head in the oven.

I had little in common with these patients. I came from a loving, upper-middle-class family, and my main exposure to drugs during my youth was when the police came to school to disseminate the Just Say No campaign. However,

I was raised on my mother's stories: born on a forest floor in Siberia while her parents fled the Nazis during World War II, enduring poverty and malnutrition during her formative years in a displaced-persons camp in Austria. I understood that I had won the jackpot in the privilege department. As undeserving as I felt of my privilege, these people seemed equally undeserving of their misfortune.

Not only did working with this population feel meaningful, it was fun. In the early 2000s, I volunteered with a group called VANDU: Vancouver Area Network of Drug Users. The first time I entered their office I felt like I was walking in to Theatre of the Absurd – heroin users nodded off around the table, while stimulant users bounced off the walls. But as I sat in the corner and observed, I was humbled and impressed as they stuck to an agenda addressing compelling issues: a health network they were forming to do alley patrols and needle exchanges, a protest they were planning to bring attention to the need for safe injection sites. They gradually became my most formidable instructors in public health and grassroots advocacy.

Their methods reflected the candour and compassion I came to expect from drug users. When a member who had been kicked off the board of directors requested to rejoin the group, it was suggested that they go around the table and have each member say how they felt about it. "Larry, you can't ask girls for sexual favours in exchange for a clean needle," one explained. I marvelled at the no-BS approach – if only such transparency existed in all groups.

They challenged me to reassess my perceptions of right and wrong. They asked me to steal supplies like Band-Aids, gloves, gauze, and needles from the hospital, and to supervise the illegal safe injection facility (SIF) they were starting (at the time the Canadian government still opposed SIFs) – a room with a single bathroom where users could inject themselves. Concerned for my reputation and license, I bought myself time by suggesting that I do some research first. After studying the literature, which showed evidence of morbidity and mortality reductions with SIFs, and having dealt with the consequences of unsafe drug use among my patients (HIV, hepatitis, severe skin infections, heart infections, overdose etc.), I realized that it would be unethical not to provide this service for people. They helped me see that just because something is a law does not make it right. Years later, the government confirmed their prescient public health measures by opening Canada's first legal SIF in Vancouver.

Amidst the suffering, I witnessed great capacity for community and relationship. Mary was a sex worker and lived in a bedbug-ridden hotel in the Downtown Eastside. Despite her outwardly depressing life, she was a ray of sunshine. Her short blond hair tufted out like a baby chick, and she had a little girl's voice and mannerisms. "Doctor Alana!" she would happily shout down the hallway when she saw me, and would run over excitedly to hug me or share news. She always thanked me for coming to the office: "It's just so amazing of you to work with us, we love you so much!" She died of AIDS in her early 40s. At her funeral, a young transgender woman cried, "When I had nowhere to go, she took me in. She taught me how to wear makeup. She was like a mother to me." For many who have never felt welcome anywhere, the Downtown Eastside is a place where they feel accepted.

The first time I felt parallels between my life and those of my patients with addiction issues, I was in my late 20s, going through a difficult breakup, unsure of the future. One day I looked at my schedule and found that I was working three jobs, and I had booked myself to work 29 out of 30 days. I couldn't face my pain, so I was drowning it in my work. My patients echoed my own thoughts, "I just feel like such a failure," and I began to resent their relapses. I left my practice and dove into an Emergency Medicine fellowship. Fast paced, not a moment to spare, saving lives, no time for weakness – the perfect field for a doctor avoiding introspection.

For so many drug users, whose stories of trauma and neglect often began in utero, and who often have untreated mental illness, drug use begins as a reprieve from suffering. Years later, my own coping strategies of escapism and perfectionism had helped me to achieve the "perfect life" I had dreamed of: I had an amazing husband, two beautiful children, and a dog, lived in a beautiful home, and worked as an ER doctor. But just as the drug user's solution eventually becomes their downfall, so my efforts to be successful caught up with me. The stress of multiple moves between countries, life changes, sleep deprivation from shift-work and babies, and a job that left no room for weakness took a toll. By the time I was diagnosed with post-partum depression after my second child, I had been experiencing anxiety and sadness for at least a year, taxing my marriage, distancing me from friends, making work an exercise in exhaustion. It took me too long to seek help, because I was ashamed. To not be enjoying my beautiful life, to not be not coping better with the stress it entailed, to be suffering from a disease that I learned I had my own stigma toward.

According to writer and addiction doctor Gabor Maté: "We lack compassion for the addict precisely because we are addicted ourselves in ways we don't want to accept and because we lack self-compassion." When I finally admitted that I needed help, I was ushered into the arms of incredibly supportive and effective care by the medical community. The most surprising thing I experienced when I opened up to my friends and colleagues about my diagnosis was how often they responded by sharing their similar struggles. Some were being treated, some were afraid to ask for help, many were self-medicating. Medical literature suggests that physicians may have higher prevalence of depression than non-physicians. In the United States, about one physician dies by suicide every day.

Self-improvement is noble and what we all strive for, but are we only loveable and worthy if we change? What if changing requires self-love?

I met Debra, who I mentioned above, in her home many years ago, when I visited her with a social worker. Formerly a hard-core injection drug user, she was off all street drugs, living in an apartment out of the DTES (Downtown Eastside), and had recently been granted custody of her child. I asked her what had made her change. She told me how, one day, when she was working the streets as a prostitute, a john assaulted her in an alley. She was so beat up that she was confined to her apartment and couldn't turn tricks. But she was still addicted to drugs, and needed money to support her habit. So, from her room, she started cutting hair for people. One day she was well enough to go downstairs, and the lady who worked at the fruit stand told her, "You know, you have a real talent for haircutting." "That moment," Debra told me, "was the first time in my life that I saw myself as something other than what my father told me I was: a ... whore. Suddenly, I was more. I was a hairdresser." It was the start of a miraculous transformation.

My own effort to practise self-compassion contributed to my husband and I moving our family back to Vancouver from the United States a year ago, closer to family, to socialized medicine, to nature. I found myself back in the DTES, working at a similar job to what I did before practising as an ER doctor, with people who have difficult lives, challenging dependencies, and mental illness. When I work with them now, I don't just see people who are suffering, I see myself, and all of us: human and fragile and needing support to thrive. And I do not feel ashamed of this. I feel connected. I feel freed.

1. Who does charity work benefit?

2. Do people who make bad choices about opioid use have anything to contribute to their communities?

"AS OPIOID EPIDEMIC CONTINUES, STEPS TO CURB IT MULTIPLY," BY CHARLES ORNSTEIN, FROM *PROPUBLICA*, MAY 12, 2016

The overdose death toll from opioids, both prescription drugs and heroin, has almost quadrupled since 1999. In 2014 alone, 28,000 people died of opioid overdoses, more than half from prescription drugs.

Just last month, public awareness of the opioid epidemic reached a new level when Prince was found dead with prescription narcotics on him and authorities began to investigate their role in his demise. In recent weeks, lawmakers and regulators have moved to augment treatment options for addiction and to require more education for doctors who prescribe opioids. The U.S. House of Representatives is voting on a package of bills this week; the Senate passed its own bill in March.

Also in that span, the Los Angeles Times has published an investigation of Purdue Pharma, the maker of the blockbuster pain pill OxyContin, and CNN held a town hallmeeting on the consequences of addiction to narcotics. Dr. David A. Kessler, former commissioner of the Food and Drug Administration, wrote an op-ed in the New York Times, calling the embrace of opioids "one of the biggest mistakes in modern medicine."

Today, ProPublica added warnings labels to the pages of narcotic drugs in our Prescriber Checkup news app, prompted by indications that some readers are using the tool to find doctors who will prescribe these drugs with few or no questions asked (See our editor's note).

The effectiveness of any of these steps remains to be seen. There is broad consensus on the need for more treatment options, more education, more careful prescribing by doctors. But there's still much debate about the details—and funding–for each of those steps.

What's clear is that in recent months there has been an increasing emphasis on the role of health providers and the agencies that oversee them to stem access to widely abused prescription drugs:

- In March, the Centers for Disease Control and Prevention released guidelines on prescribing of opioids for chronic pain, defined as pain that lasts for more than three months (excluding pain related to cancer, end-of-life and palliative care.) The guidelines call on doctors to choose therapies other than opioids as their preferred option; to use the lowest possible doses; and to monitor all patients closely.
- That same month, the FDA announced tougher warning labels on immediate-release opioids, such as fentanyl, hydrocodone, and oxycodone, to note the "serious risks of misuse, abuse, addiction, overdose and death."
- Nonprofit groups and medical experts in April asked the federal Centers for Medicare and Medicaid Services to remove questions about pain control from a survey of hospital patients' satisfaction to remove any incentive to overtreat pain. And they asked The Joint Commission, which accredits health facilities, to revise its standards to deemphasize "unnecessary, unhelpful and unsafe pain treatments." The commission pushed back, saying its standards do no such thing.

Just yesterday, Dr. Steven J. Stack, president of the American Medical Association, called on doctors to do more. He encouraged doctors to use their state's Prescription Drug Monitoring Program to ensure their patients aren't shopping for multiple doctors to prescribe them drugs. He called on them to co-prescribe a rescue drug, naloxone, to patients at risk of overdose. And he told them to generally avoid starting opioids for new patients with chronic, non-cancer pain.

"As physicians, we are on the front lines of an opioid epidemic that is crippling communities across the country," Stack wrote in a statement, published on the Huffington Post. "We must accept and embrace our professional responsibility to treat our patients' pain without worsening the current crisis. These are actions we must take as physicians individually and collectively to do our part to end this epidemic."

1. What are some recent actions that have been taken, according to this article, to end the opioid epidemic?

"HOW MY ACID REFLUX NEARLY LED TO AN OVERDOSE," BY ALIYYA, FROM *ABOVE THE INFLUENCE*, MARCH 13, 2016

I'm a senior in college and have been interning with the Partnership for Drug-Free Kids for almost a year, and yet even I had an uncomfortably close call with prescription painkillers. Without the intervention of a friend's mother, my story could have become another tragic example of the Rx to Heroin pipeline. And it all started with a bad case of acid reflux.

The acid reflux was actually a symptom of gallstones, and after two attacks in one week, I was told that I needed surgery to remove my gall bladder. I am an international student, so with no family here in the US, my friends accompanied me to the hospital. After surgery I was discharged with a prescription for medicine I had never heard of before. I had it filled the following day as I was in extreme pain. The directions said to allow four hours in between each dose, as required. My friends and I translated this to mean that I *had* to take a dosage every four hours.

Hence I started taking Percocet (Oxycodone) every four hours for two days on an empty stomach (I had lost my appetite due to the gas pumped into my stomach to aid the surgery). My friend, doing her best to be helpful and take care of me, had a timer on her phone and would remind me to take my medicine. Pain or no pain, I kept taking the pills.

Never having dealt with a medical situation by myself before, I assumed these pills were good for me and would not only help me with the pain, but also heal me somehow. I was given no instructions by my doctor or nurses on what this medication was for, how to use it properly or what the consequences of misuse could be. Even though the medicine helped me with the pain, after two days I was unable to open my eyes or even move from the bed. A friend's mother came and picked me up the evening of the second day and told me to stop taking the medicine immediately.

An hour after skipping my dosage my body started shaking and I started feeling nausea. I threw up multiple times that night and could not close my eyes due to dizziness. My head would spin in circles if I tried to sleep for more than five minutes. After consulting with a family doctor, it was determined that my body was going through withdrawal. I had all the symptoms an addicted person experiences in the initial stages of denying their body of the substance it has become used to consuming.

This was when I found out the medicine I had been taking is extremely addictive, and even though it subdued my pain, it did more damage than good. Oxycodone has one of the highest rates of addiction in America and many of those addictions began with a legal prescription just like mine.

The doctors, nurses and even the pharmacist provided no warning about the potential side effects. I was never told that these are highly addictive pills. There were minimal instructions on the pill bottle and no mention on the discharge form of how this medication should be used with caution. Plus, I was given 30 pills! It only took SEVEN pills before I experienced withdrawal symptoms.

Had someone better informed not intervened, I could have finished the 30 pills within only four days, and overdose would have been a real risk. Symptoms of an opioid overdose include depressed respiration, extreme drowsiness progressing to stupor or coma, muscle flaccidity and cardiac arrest that can lead to death. I was fortunate that someone recognized the danger I was in, and acted quickly.

My own naivety of the medication I was being prescribed is a little embarrassing given the circumstances. But my friends were just as naive, and given the statistics on opioid addiction, so are a lot of other people! It's estimated that between 26.4 and 36 million people abuse opioids worldwide. It's disconcerting how easily I could have become a statistic.

My experience highlights a lot of flaws in the system. But until more changes are in place, the most important thing you can do is to educate yourself and others.

1. How can a person obey a prescription yet still have problems with a medication?

2. What can a person do to participate in her or his health care when using prescription drugs?

"YOUR CHRONIC PAIN: AN OWNER'S MANUAL," BY BARBARA GEIGER, FROM *BARBARA GEIGER.ME*, NOVEMBER 11, 2016

When it comes to acute trauma, the damage is obvious. The broken leg is at a bad angle, the blood is pouring out of somewhere, or multi-coloured bruises radiate from where the damage was done. Hospitals are equipped to handle it. Doctors are trained to manage it. People comprehend it. There are cures and solutions for acute pain with a clear end point.

Chronic pain, on the other hand, isn't well understood. Doctors can't fix it. Surgeries often make it worse. Society either doesn't understand it or puts their own baggage on top of it as though it were a trolley. Chronic pain doesn't have a cure, the solutions are often worse than the problem itself and the best possible outcome involves accepting your new normal, not trying to change it.

It's been more than ten years since I reached for my toothbrush one morning and realized that my left index finger was numb, as though I had slept on it but nothing else on my hand. I went with the folk cure of leaving it alone and hoping it gets better, but my doctor didn't seem too worried. Four months later, I woke up with shooting pain down my arm so bad that I couldn't sit up. Any part my left arm could bend radiated pain.

When you have pain, the doctor is trained to use the pain scale. Zero being no pain at all, ten being the worst pain imaginable. There's no litmus paper or formula that comes up with that number; it's self-reported. For acute pain, it makes a lot of sense in an emergency situation, but for chronic pain, it's next to useless. Obviously everyone's ten is subjective, but I spent my active youth crashing from one accident to the next. I've crashed into the ditch trying to make an S turn with an open throttle on a bike. I've had a horse pile drive me into the dirt at a dead gallop. I've fallen down a mountainside with a ski that didn't pop off the way it should have, almost ripping off my foot as I fell. I had a man bash my face in with his fists to the point that one eye completely swelled shut and the other only open a sliver.

Compared to that pain, what I experience on the day-to-day is a three or four at best. But that's for acute pain, not pain that goes on and on and on. And on and on and on. I'd keep going, but this article has a word limit. Chronic pain is the squeal of a brake pad telling you it needs to be fixed but in a world where there is no replacement parts. It leaves you gutted and gasping for air on the pier of life. Instead of a simple line scale, a three-dimensional chess board is needed.

Finding a doctor willing to help can be a major struggle. I found life got easier once I had a diagnosis, but the eighteen months that passed between me waking up in agony and some technician looking at my results and saying I had the MRI of someone sixty years my senior was miserable. My doctor was a very nice lady, but she spoke out of both sides of her mouth. She would say that she believed me and would do all that she could to help and then tell me that I was much too young to have that much pain. Worse, while the pain manifested itself in my arm, the damage was done in my neck. So for the first year they were looking at the arm from the shoulder down. Since there was nothing wrong with my arm, all the ultrasounds, Xrays and conduction tests came back negative.

Some doctors will try to believe you. Others won't give you the benefit of the doubt. Scheduling the MRI took six months and before I could have one done, our family doctor moved away. One of the interim doctors told me I had tennis elbow. When I asked why it was that my shoulder hurt if it was in my elbow, he templed his fingers and said, "Ooooh, so it's your **shoulder** that hurts now?" in an obvious "gotcha" tone. A week later the MRI results came in and the damage to my neck was obvious, but I'll never forget how helpless I felt in that moment.

I'm in a much better place now and I'll get to how I got there in a moment, but you can't talk about chronic pain without talking about the medications involved in treating it. They're currently working on a painkiller derived from a particular spider's venom. It's completely non-addictive or euphoric and if it's strong enough to allow a spider to liquefy your insides and suck them up through their fangs without kicking up much of a fuss, it should manage chronic conditions, but that's years away.

For right now we have opiates and opioids. Conventional wisdom used to say that pain patients using their medications correctly only have a 2% chance of addiction. Recent studies have brought that number up to 35%. More people die of prescription medication abuse than they do from any other form of opiate. Purdue, the company that makes OxyContin, lied to the doctors about not only the addiction rate but also the length of time the pills were effective. After selling medical grade heroin for so long, they then switched the formula so that they couldn't be tampered with and while on paper that sounds like a good thing, it's the reason why you now know what fentanyl is and how high its butcher's bill costs.

So finding a pain specialist who cares about finding the dose that allows you function day-to-day with a clear

189

head is vitally important to both your health and your well-being. The solution to managing pain is not going to be found in a prescription bottle with endless refills, but proper pain management will greatly improve your quality of life. Pain levels and your emotional state go hand in hand, so if an anti-depressant helps with that, give it a chance.

Back in elementary school the teachers used to hand out those morbid life or severe injury insurance pamphlets for us to take home. We poured over them, trying to figure out exactly what we could lose that would impact our lives the least but pay out the most money. Losing your thumb, for example, earned you ten grand while losing an index finger was slightly less and losing your pinky was barely worth breaking out the hacksaw. The naïve idea that there was anything more valuable than health was beyond us.

It's easy to fall into the trap that allows the pain to define you. Chronic pain can challenge the most optimistic outlook on life. It can test the best relationship and alter your path from where you thought you were going to be to where you end up. The surgery that might be able to fix the constricted nerve channel and shave off the bone spurs has a one percent mortality chance, and another one percent chance of either being a paraplegic or a quadriplegic. Both specialists I've seen have assured me that the risk/reward is just too high. I've also talked a lot of people who went the surgery route, and not one of them would happily go back to the amount of pain they were in before the surgery. One person had five corrective surgeries to correct the first one, and her pain level was exponentially increased. With so many nerves and blood vessels located at C3 and C4, the best the specialists could say was take the pills, try not to get too addicted, and come back in a decade to see if there were any advances on the procedure.

But the drugs are just one of the tools I've used to greatly enhance my quality of life. Studies of children in hospitals have shown that being creative is as effective for dealing with the pain as some opiates. Being a writer, I can attest to this. When the pain is out of control, simply being in a far off land in my head works better than handfuls of medication. Meditation, yoga, hobbies, anything that takes your mind off the pain can raise your pain threshold. I pace myself using the Spoon Theory, https://en.wikipedia.org/wiki/Spoon_theory − a brilliant way to visualize your new normal. While I have the objectively greatest partner in the world, being your own self-advocate and speaking up for yourself is vital. Assembling the right Team You makes all the difference in the world. From your doctors to the pharmacist to your friends or your therapist should all be on your side. You don't have room in your life for people who aren't there to make the world a better place.

At the start of this journey, I wanted to take enough pills that I could close my eyes and wake up when the pain's gone. I lost three years of my life to pharmaceutical zombification. Life will continue, and the sooner I accepted that this was my new normal, the happier I've been. Chronic pain does what it says on the tin, but in the long list of things that make up who you are and what you're going to be, it is not your main ingredient.

1. How can people participate in their own health care, with or without using opioids?

"VETERANS RETURN HOME TO FACE ANOTHER KIND OF BATTLE," BY FORREST BURNSON, FROM *NEWS21*, AUGUST 24, 2013

Alcohol is the most widely abused substance among post-9/11 veterans of the wars in Iraq and Afghanistan, according to several reports reviewed by News21.

The extent of other substance abuse — particularly prescription drugs — is not entirely known. While several reports paint different pictures, the increasing number of active-duty soldiers and veterans who are being prescribed potentially dangerous drugs is a cause for concern for some veteran health professionals.

"The current generation of veterans faces a much more dangerous and wider array of substances that are readily available," said Andrew Saxon, a psychiatrist at the Department of Veterans Affairs hospital in Seattle, Wash. His specialty is addiction and substance abuse.

A 2010 study by the VA found that 21.8 percent of male and 4.7 percent of female Iraq and Afghanistan veterans abused alcohol. Yet a 2012 study sponsored by the VA and published in the American Journal of Public Health — using the same survey questions — found the rate of alcohol abuse among Iraq and Afghanistan veterans to be 41.4 percent for men and 17.0 percent for women. That study noted "this discrepancy might suggest that the context of the VA clinical setting could lead veterans to underreport their drinking in routine screening, resulting in underestimates of the severity of the problem."

Changing the way the survey is taken could help, one researcher said.

"In the actual clinic, people might be reluctant to admit to having alcohol problems," said Sue Eisen, author of the 2012 study and principal investigator at the Bedford VA hospital outside Boston, Mass., "and that was why we might have found a higher rate of alcohol problems. Our survey was much more anonymous."

Alcohol was the primary substance of abuse for 50.7 percent of veterans ages 21 to 39 seeking treatment in non-VA hospitals. That compares to 34.4 percent of non-veterans, according to a 2012 report by the federal Center for Behavioral Health Statistics and Quality.

Six percent of veterans from Operation Enduring Freedom in Afghanistan and from Operation Iraqi Freedom who enrolled in VA health care reported suffering from alcohol dependence and 5 percent suffer from other drug abuse, according to a 2013 Congressional Research Service report. However, many of them may have avoided reporting alcohol or substance abuse, and about half of Iraq and Afghanistan veterans are not enrolled in VA health care, according to the Congressional Research report.

Similarly, Eisen found in her study that 3 percent of Iraq and Afghanistan veterans suffer from drug abuse, though she noted that her survey had a small, self-selecting sample of veterans.

The military began cracking down on illicit drugs in 1981, when urine tests were mandated for all personnel. Illicit drug use detected by urinalysis among active-duty soldiers hovered around 1 percent between 2007 and 2011, compared to a self-reported rate of nearly 28 percent in 1980, according to a 2011 Department of Defense report. The Pentagon examined only 20 percent of urine samples for opiates such as oxycodone, codeine, morphine and oxymorphone. The Defense Department mandated in 2004 that all drug tests would screen for heroin, because of concerns over deployments in Afghanistan, the largest producer of poppies, the plant that yields heroin. Beginning in 2012, Pentagon screenings tested troops for hydrocodone, a derivative of codeine and the primary ingredient in Vicodin, and other common pain medications.

For one vet, the battle continued at home — with the bottle.

After three days of drinking, Scott Branscum was able to sleep for a few hours. When he awoke, the 35-year-old former Air Force flight medic mistakenly thought someone had broken into his house. He grabbed a loaded shotgun, yelling at his fiance to hide in the garage and call the police. After he cleared every room in the house, his fiance sat him down. Something was wrong.

Branscum had returned in 2008 from deployment in Iraq. Initially happy to be home, his war experiences, however, were setting in. The nightmares proved so unbearable that he turned to drinking.

"I knew it, but I hadn't realized it. I knew deep down inside that something was going on," he said. "If you drink enough, you don't have nightmares."

While alcohol is used most when veterans self-medicate, the rising use of prescription pain relief in the military and the VA system has prompted calls for change. For example, pain-reliever prescriptions written by military physicians quadrupled to nearly 3.8 million between 2001 and 2009, according to the National Institute on Drug Abuse.

That increase was cause for concern in the military. In 2009, Eric Schoomaker, then-surgeon general of the Army, led a task force comprising all services and the VA to address the issue. The resulting 2010 report found that "pain medications are relatively inexpensive, patients readily accept their use, and they require minimum time expenditure on behalf of the provider and patient," but that "the possible over-reliance on medications to treat pain has other unintended consequences, however, such as an increase in prescription medication abuse."

"What we see nationally now is a problem with overuse of opioids and prescription narcotics, (which) is occurring in the military as well," Schoomaker said in a News21 interview.

Some VA doctors and mental health professionals are concerned about increasingly long-term prescriptions for opioid painkillers, which include Oxycontin and Vicodin.

"That increased use has occurred despite any available empirical data showing their effectiveness in treating chronic pain," said Ben Morasco, a VA clinical psychologist in Portland, Ore., noting that there have not been any long-term studies of the effects of prescription painkillers.

Yet many veterans who have wounds that might require prescription painkillers might also have psychological wounds, such as post-traumatic stress disorder, which can increase the likelihood of substance abuse. According to the VA, one-fifth of veterans diagnosed with PTSD also have a substance-use disorder.

Injured soldiers "are coming back and they're being discharged and then resuming services in the community or the VA, and they've been taking medications for multiple years. And we don't really know how safe that is. That needs to be determined," Morasco said.

Alcohol and substance abuse play a major role in putting soldiers and veterans at risk for suicide. In one study conducted by the Army in 2010, 45 percent of non-fatal suicide attempts from 2005 and 2009 involved alcohol and drugs.

Realizing he had a problem, Branscum sought treatment and was diagnosed as having PTSD. He checked in to the PTSD clinic at the VA hospital in Little Rock, Ark., where he joined other veterans who struggled with similar issues. Though a welcoming environment, Branscum said there was a culture of drug abuse among some patients.

"They were abusing drugs to the point where they were jeopardizing other patients' progress," he said, referring to prescription drugs. "It was everywhere. I could have purchased whatever I wanted within 15 minutes of being there."

Some patients in the clinic continued down that path. Others checked themselves out within days of being there. But Branscum turned his life around.

"It was actually amazing. I credit me being the kind of person I am today from a lot of things I learned there," he said.

"There's that mentality of, 'I don't need to ask for help with this.' It's hard to admit to your family members and loved ones when you actually do need help because they have this picture of you in their mind of this tough guy who can handle anything," he said.

"When in reality, you're a human like everyone else."

1. Why are veterans particularly susceptible to opioid abuse?

2. What other populations might be vulnerable to becoming addicted to opioids?

"ADDICTS SAY THEY ARE TRAPPED IN A VICIOUS CYCLE OF DEPENDENCE," BY LILY ALTAVENA, *CRONKITE NEWS*, JANUARY 5, 2017

TUCSON – They pawned their wedding rings, lost their house and nearly walked away from their marriage. For almost a decade, their world revolved around prescription pills and, later, heroin.

He stopped working. Her depression spiraled. Their lives narrowed to one purpose: staving off the sickness that sets in during opioid withdrawal.

The addiction morphed into an uncontrollable obsession, starting with Brian Parker's motorcycle accident in 2007. The father of four suffered nerve damage after he was T-boned at a Tucson intersection. Trying to hold onto his job as a welder, Parker said he could not go a day without the morphine and oxycodone doctors prescribed him. His wife, Jamie Dutton, was having headaches, so she started taking pills, too.

"Every day I woke up, I was sick, so before you even get out of bed, you're looking for your pill bottle," Dutton said. "And it's a vicious cycle. You're afraid to even leave the house without looking to see if you have enough medication. ... It's a scary feeling."

In Arizona, drug users say they are gripped by an almost-identical pattern of drug addiction, which starts with a pill bottle and ends with a needle.

Cronkite News conducted a four-month investigation into the rise of prescription opioid abuse in Arizona. In 2015, more than 2 million grams of oxycodone alone came into the state, the third-highest total per capita in the country.

Dozens of journalists at Arizona State University examined thousands of records and traveled across the state to interview addicts, law enforcement, public officials and health care experts. The goal: uncover the root of the epidemic, explain the ramifications and provide solutions.

Since 2010, more than 3,600 people have overdosed and died from opioids in Arizona. In 2015, the dead numbered 701 – the highest of any year before, according to an analysis by the Arizona Department of Health Services.

Every single addict Cronkite News interviewed said they never expected that popping legal pain medications would seduce them into an insatiable cycle of drug abuse. These addicts are young men who relapse fresh out of rehab in Prescott, women who leave their children behind in search of recovery and sons from close-knit families with mothers who, in their words, love them "almost" to death.

According to a 2016 report from the U.S. Surgeon General, 12.5 million people across the United States said they had misused prescription pain relievers in the past year.

"Abusing a prescription opioid is no different than putting heroin in your arm, in my opinion," said Lt. James Scott, deputy commander of the Tucson Police Department's Counter Narcotics Alliance. "They're both opioids. You're taking them for the wrong reason. It doesn't matter that a doctor prescribed them to you, it doesn't make it right."

Dutton and Parker, together for almost 20 years, are in recovery. They have four children, two dogs and a turtle that crawls around the tile floor in their cramped house. They are tenants in their house – one in a long string of rentals they have lived in as addiction drained their bank accounts.

The pet turtle that wanders the tile floor first belonged to Dutton's mother, who left it behind after she fatally overdosed on fentanyl and oxycodone in November 2010. Julia Barnett was a nurse. She rescued animals. She loved her children. She was also a drug addict.

One of her doctors was Robert Osborne, an anesthesiologist who prescribed her hundreds of pain pills. She freely shared those drugs with Dutton and her husband, as well as her 41-year-old son, who died of heroin and alcohol intoxication last year.

Four years after Barnett's death, a federal grand jury in 2014 indicted Osborne for prescribing thousands of painkillers to patients across Tucson. Osborne pleaded not guilty to all the charges in the indictment, which included unlawful distribution and dispensing of a controlled substance, maintaining a drug-involved premises and health care fraud. That case is ongoing.

"It caused a whirlwind of addiction in my family," Dutton said.

Parker also went to Osborne. He said that the doctor only took cash, stripped him naked, asked if he was with the Drug Enforcement Administration. When Parker said no, "then he asks you what you want, and you tell him, and he writes it out."

"He was just a legalized dope dealer," he said. "He is somewhat responsible for what happened to my mother-in-law."

Parker soon lost his job and his health insurance, and he turned from pills to heroin. He said he had no choice. The sickness from withdrawal was so strong, it was like "God revoked your soul and then you got hit by a truck," he said.

Three out of four new heroin users said they used prescription opioids before they moved on to shooting, smoking or snorting heroin, according to the Centers for Disease Control and Prevention. Nearly every addict interviewed by Cronkite News told their own version of that same story.

Dutton said she has been sober for about a year. Parker has been clean since August. He said he is trying to be a better father to his two younger sons and two older daughters who grew up in the shadow of his addiction.

"They see me as a piece-of-s--- addict," he said. "They deserve better. But I'm trying now."

Dutton said they recently found empty heroin bags in their 17-year-old daughter's room.

"She knows all the dealers in this neighborhood, and we don't want her to go down that route," she said.

KAYLA MCBRIDE

When she didn't have money to buy pills, Kayla McBride would sleep with her dealer, a man she found through mutual friends on Facebook. She was looking for Percocet, a drug she was introduced to at 16 years old.

"I didn't care, because I was really sick, and I said OK," she said. "And I mean I felt disgusting about myself, but he handed me the pills and I did them right there and then, broad daylight, pulled out a foil and started smoking them."

McBride said she overdosed five times. The 23 year old was in a sober living home in Prescott in September, but by November she had relapsed. What started as a high school pill habit morphed into a full-blown heroin addiction.

"Once you have experienced the high of meth, heroin, pills, anything like that, it's always gonna be with you," she said.

Two weeks after McBride graduated from high school, she met Brandon, now her ex-boyfriend. He introduced her to heroin.

"I just wanted to feel how he was feeling," she said.

Drugs colored their relationship. The first year she used heroin, he would shoot her up because she was afraid of needles. One day, she learned how to shoot herself up. She said she didn't want to have to wait for him.

McBride has been trying to get clean since 2013, relapsing over and over again. Family members have stopped talking to her. She has a 13-year-old brother who has known her only in the throes of addiction.

Like McBride, nearly every addict relapses. The rate of recovery from substance abuse among adolescents is 35 percent, the U.S. Surgeon General reports. Achieving long-term recovery – if achieved at all – can take as long as eight or nine years.

"It's that little ... that voice in the back of your head telling you one more time: It's OK, it's OK," McBride said. "But one time, it's never enough, ever."

NICOLE CREECH

Nicole Creech said she started using prescription painkillers at a young age to feel "normal."

Eventually, she began experimenting with other drugs, from ecstasy to heroin to crystal meth.

Now, 16 months sober, she said her recovery from addiction is still an active part of her life — one that takes work, patience and strength.

"I have two options," Creech said. "I either stay and do this every day, whether I'm in pain, sad or extremely happy. Or I go out there, and I die. I truly believe that addiction only has one word for me left — and that's death."

BROCK BEVELL

Brock Bevell stared at the neat rows of orange pill bottles lined up in his medicine cabinet. In that one moment, he realized he cared more about the contents of the cabinet than his marriage. Maybe even more than his kids. He decided to detox.

For seven long days, he said he lay, detoxing, on the bathroom floor.

"That kind of triggered me like, 'OK, so you have this addiction, Brock,'" he said. "'You care more about your pills than anything around you.' So my family suffered, my job suffered, my relationship suffered with other people. Everything suffered from it."

Bevell, then a Mesa police officer, was a father of five devoted to his Mormon faith. He didn't drink alcohol or do drugs until he started racking up injuries as a police officer. It started with a blown knee after hopping a fence in pursuit of a suspect. In another pursuit, a suspect high on meth ran him over with a car.

His cabinets were filled with Percocet, Vicodin, hydrocodone and more from different doctors.

"I had a ridiculous amount of drugs in my house," he said. "Because I was a police officer, the doctor never felt like, 'hey, this guy's doctor shopping.'"

His marriage dissolved. His addiction crescendoed. He retired from the police department.

Bevell has been sober for seven years. He moved to Show Low, where he worked in the medical examiner's office and as an assistant principal at the local high school, where he saw parents staggering into the school high or drunk.

Last year, he and his brother Jimmy opened Blue Vase Recovery Center, one of the few treatment centers in Navajo County.

"In my mind, pills are so easy," Bevell said. "Pills are everywhere. Every medicine cabinet in the United States has pills."

BRETT MORRISON

Brett Morrison, a graduate of Brophy College Preparatory in Phoenix, said he started devouring pills the summer before he started college at Northern Arizona University. In high school, he smoked marijuana almost every day, and tried cocaine and ecstasy. But painkillers felt different.

"It was like, 'This is what I've been missing my whole life,'" he said. "It felt as if I had a spiritual experience at that moment."

Morrison, now 34, didn't finish college. Instead, his life was all about the drugs.

"I've been to 11 rehabs," he said. "I've been to prison twice. I have lost a countless amount of friends. I have spent hundreds of thousands of dollars. I have lost businesses. I have lost my integrity. I have lost my self-worth."

His mother, Janice Morrison, said she was afraid of her son, no longer recognizing the "wonderful, joyful, energetic, smart, bright child" she had raised. Now, he was often high on painkillers or heroin, verbally abusive or in too much of a daze to get out of bed.

"He was not Brett at all," she said. "And when he was high, like anyone that's walked through this, their loved one becomes a monster."

Surgery on an injured shoulder made the problem worse. Even when he told a surgeon he was a drug addict, Morrison walked out of the hospital with a prescription for 30 OxyContin pills, his mother remembers.

The amount of oxycodone prescribed in the United States accounts for 81 percent of the world's consumption of the drug, according to the National Institute on Drug Abuse.

"What's unique about prescription drugs and opioid drugs is it's within our own health care community and that's unique. Unique in the sense that you can go to your local pharmacy and get these drugs," said Steven Duplissis, chief counsel of the Arizona Attorney General's health care fraud and abuse section. "You can get a prescription written by a physician and again the important factor is there needs to be a legitimate medical purpose for the prescription to be written."

Morrison said he eventually turned to the street to buy pills, sometimes spending as much as $300 a day. At one point, he had the phone numbers of eight or nine dealers on his phone. At 28, he moved to heroin. It was cheaper.

"Anybody who tells me that they'll never stick a needle in their arm eventually does, that's just the progression of the disease as far as I've seen," he said.

He overdosed on heroin and almost died the night before his brother's wedding. Morrison was the best man.

"That didn't keep me sober," he said. "Just the fact that I see people dying all around me does not keep me sober. But it scares me today."

He has been sober for more than nine months. He helps other addicts at a sober living house in Scottsdale.

"All I cared about was myself, what I can get from you, how I can use any bit of my intellect my humor to try to manipulate you and persuade you in order to get something I wanted," he said of his addiction.

EMILY SHY

She says she was born "horse crazy." As a kid, Emily Shy begged her parents to buy her a horse. She trained the animals, groomed them and competed with them.

But it was the aches and pains from doing what she loved that drove her to an unruly addiction, which eventually took her away from the comforting routine of saddling up and riding.

Shy did demanding work as a horse wrangler in South Phoenix. She estimates unloading 10 bales of hay by herself the day she had a back spasm that sent her to the doctor. For one month, she said they prescribed her 180 Percocet, along with a muscle relaxant.

"You get handed two scripts for 90 Percocets a piece, it's really, I don't know, it's hard not to get hooked on them," she said. "I started feeling like I needed the pills just to function."

The CDC estimates that medical professionals prescribe opioids to one out of five patients with non-cancer pain or with pain-related diagnoses: injuries from car accidents, athletics, on-the-job mishaps and more. From 1999 to 2010, prescription opioid overdose deaths of women in the U.S. increased by 400 percent.

In 2011, Shy flipped her car leaving a bar called Cocomo Joe's in Cave Creek, after popping pills the entire day. The car was totaled. She walked away without a scratch and was placed on house arrest for 75 days.

"At first, you have all this energy and you're just so happy and all this other stuff and then it switches and you're tired and falling asleep and by that time you're addicted," she said. "You don't have much of a choice at that point because if you do, you'll get sick."

She stopped working with horses.

She was 24 when she first started taking pills. At 28, she started on meth. It was an arrest in 2013 that motivated Shy to get sober. Her boyfriend at the time was sent to prison. She was pregnant.

"They (law enforcement) ran a drug test because I had admitted that I was on stuff," she said. "It came back … the drug panel came back with 17 different substances. Heroin being one. Pills being another."

Getting sober has been "confusing and hard." She's relapsed on pills after dental work. After one 90-day program, she remembers a craving for drugs so intense, she said she returned to using for at least six more months. Her parents, she said, were heartbroken.

"It makes zero sense, the things we do and the things that drive us to do the things we do," she said. "The normal person says, 'oh you just stop, just quit, just make up your mind.' But it's not that easy, once that chemical takes a hold of you."

Shy hopes to be an accountant. She's on track to graduate with an associate's degree in May. She's raising her daughter, Chloe.

"To be in recovery, it means giving back to my community and trying to help other people that have the disease of addiction," she said.

Cronkite News reporters Kate Peifer and Karla Liriano contributed to this article.

1. What is most surprising to you in these personal stories about opioid addiction?

2. How did these addicts first begin to use opioids?

CONCLUSION

It is distressing to consider whether opioid abuse has been recognized as an epidemic in recent years only because the dead now include not only marginalized people, but people with homes and families. "The assumption is that these deaths are happening among junkies, but that is very, very wrong," says Dr. Benedikt Fischer, a senior scientist at the Center for Addiction and Mental Health in Toronto. "The people who are dying are not street users; they are being introduced to these drugs medically."[1] No worker is more than one injury away from needing pain relief in order to keep earning a living.

Opinions are being expressed in newspapers and social media that the so-called opioid epidemic is not so much about the increased use of opioids since 2010 but about the use of opioids by white people of working age, outside the downtown core of cities. "Step outside of the city, and the suicide rate among young people … doubles," writes David Wong, executive editor of *Cracked*. "The recession pounded rural communities, but all the recovery went to the cities … To [rural communities], it seems like the plight of poor minorities [in urban ghettos] is only used as a club to bat away white cries for help. Meanwhile, the rate of rural white suicides and overdoses skyrockets."[2]

Another opinion written by Olga Kazan in *The Atlantic* magazine states that "not only are middle-aged white people drinking more, using more opioids, and killing themselves at higher rates, more of them are getting sick with the diseases that usually kill older people. And when they do get sick, they don't get better." Kazan quotes CDC statistics and studies showing that some middle-aged white Americans have been falling behind economically, and suffering as minorities do from "broader societal problems that have deleterious health effects" and from "weakened communal institutions."[3]

Community-wide interventions are also recommended by a criminologist at Simon Fraser University. "I think it's important we look at different ways of dealing with addiction that are non-criminal," says Neil Boyd.[4] Though judges should consider the fentanyl epidemic when making sentencing decisions, that's not the best solution, he believes. Many non-violent drug users might be more appropriately handled through health care and through improvements to entire communities and states, rather than criminal charges and prison.

Where government services are not meeting their needs, addicts and their families and friends are forming *ad hoc* support groups, such as Team Recovery, which started up in Toledo, Ohio. Their vision statement is shared by many community groups and charities:

Less Death

Less Crime

Less Drugs

Less Stigma

More Recovery

More Love[5]

BIBLIOGRAPHY

"A New Abuse-Deterrent Opioid – Xtampza ER." *The Medical Letter on Drugs and Therapeutics*, Vol. 58 (1497): 77-78. June 20, 2016. http://secure.medicalletter.org/w1497a

"AAN: Risks of Opioids Outweigh Benefits for Headache, Low Back Pain, Other Conditions." *American Academy of Neurology*, September 29, 2014. https://www.aan.com/PressRoom/Home /PressRelease/1310.

Alexander, G.C., Frattaroli, S. and Gielen, A.C., eds. "Executive Summary." *The Prescription Opioid Epidemic: An Evidence-Based Approach*. Baltimore, MD: Johns Hopkins Bloomberg School of Public Health, 2015. http://www.jhsph.edu/research/centers-and-institutes/center-for-drug-safety-and-effectiveness /opioid-epidemic-town-hall-2015/2015-prescription-opioid -epidemic-report.pdf.

Aliyya. "How My Acid Reflux Nearly Led to an Overdose." *Above the Influence*, March 13, 2016. Retrieved September 8, 2016. http://abovetheinfluence.com/reflux-overdose.

Assistant Secretary for Public Affairs. "About the Epidemic." *US Department of Health & Human Services*, June 23, 2016. http:// www.hhs.gov/opioids/about-the-epidemic.

Attaventa, Lily. "Addicts Say They are Trapped in a Vicious Cycle of Dependence." *Cronkite News*, January 5, 2017. https:// cronkitenews.azpbs.org/hookedrx/opioid-pill-addiction-cycle.

Burnson, Forrest. "Veterans Return Home to Face Another Kind of Battle." *News21*, August 24, 2013. http://backhome.news21 .com/article/drugs.

Cluff, Brayden. "Comment on 'What's the Worst Thing.'" *Reddit*, December 18, 2011. https://www.reddit.com/r/AskReddit/com- ments/nh45p/gynecologists_of_reddit_whats_the_worst_thing /c391ru0.

Columbus, Courtney. "Substance-Abuse Treatment Industry Grows to Keep Up With Demand." *Cronkite News*, January 5, 2017. https://cronkitenews.azpbs.org/hookedrx/opioid-drug -abuse-treatment-rehab-industry-growth-az.

Engelbert, Stephen. "An Unintended Side Effect of Transpar- ency." *ProPublica*, May 12, 2016. https://www.propublica.org /article/an-unintended-side-effect-of-transparency.

Geiger, Barb. "Your Chronic Pain: An Owner's Manual." *Barbara Geiger.me*, November 11, 2016. https://barbarageiger .me/2016/11/11/your-chronic-pain-an-owners-manual.

Gladden, R. Matthew, Pedro Martinez, and Puja Seth. "Fentanyl Law Enforcement Submissions and Increases in Synthetic

Opioid–Involved Overdose Deaths – 27 States, 2013–2014." *Morbidity and Mortality Weekly Report*, Centers for Disease Control, August 26, 2016. https://www.cdc.gov/mmwr/volumes/65 /wr/mm6533a2.htm.

"HHS Awards $53 Million to Help Address Opioid Epidemic." *US Department of Health & Human Services*, August 31, 2016. https://www.hhs.gov/about/news/2016/08/31/hhs-awards-53 -million-to-help-address-opioid-epidemic.html.

Hirsh, Alana. "The Need For Compassion." *Globe and Mail*, September 1, 2016. http://www.theglobeandmail.com/life /health-and-fitness/health/why-should-we-take-care-of-drug -addicts-because-like-all-of-us-they-need-support-tothrive /article31672781.

The International Adhesions Society. "The Opioid Survey." "Mind Over Matter: Prescription Pain Medications (Opioids)." *National Institute for Drug Abuse For Teachers*, 1997/2014. https:// teens.drugabuse.gov/teachers/mind-over-matter/opioids.

McCauley, Lauren. "Big Pharma's 'Stranghehold' on Congress Worsening Opioid Epidemic: Former DEA Official Tells the Guardian How Hundreds of Millions are Being Spent to Protest Pharmaceutical Industry." *Common Dreams*, October 31, 2016. http://www.commondreams.org/news/2016/10/31 /big-pharmas-stranglehold-congress-worsening -opioid-epidemic.

Morlion, Bart. "EU Aims To Avoid Opioid Epidemic." *Healthcare In Europe*, February 11, 2016. http://www.healthcare-in-europe .com/en/article/15760-eu-aims-to-avoid-opioid-epidemic.html.

Nuttall, Jeremy J. "Fentanyl Crackdown Could Bring Deadlier Drugs, Expert Says." *The Tyee*, September 1, 2016. http://thetyee.ca/News/2016/09/01/Fentanyl-Crack- down-Could-Bring-Deadlier-Drugs.

"Opioid Addiction 2016 Facts & Figures." *American Society of Addiction Medicine*. http://www.asam.org/docs/default-source /advocacy/opioid-addiction-disease-facts-figures.pdf.

Ornstein, Charles. "As Opioid Epidemic Continues, Steps to Curb It Multiply." *ProPublica,* May 12, 2016. https://www.propublica .org/article/as-opioid-epidemic-continues-steps-to-curb -it-multiply.

_____. "How the Nation's Opioid Epidemic is Morphing—and Growing." *ProPublica*, October 3, 2016. https://www .propublica.org/podcast/item/how-the-nations-opioid-epidem- ic-is-morphing-and-growing.

"Perspectives on Drugs: Trends in Heroin Use in Europe: What Do Treatment Demand Data Tell Us?" *European Drug Report 2016*, European Monitoring Centre for Drugs and Drug Addiction, May 28, 2013. http://www.emcdda.europa.eu/topics/pods/trends-in-heroin-use.

Philip, Agnel and Emily L. Mahoney. "Arizona Medical Boards Can Take Years to Penalize Doctors Who Overprescribe." *Cronkite News*, January 5, 2017. https://cronkitenews.azpbs.org/hookedrx/az-penalize-doctors-overprescribe-opioids.

Sandler, Gabriel. "Officials Try to Stop Fake Prescriptions, But Addicts Remain Persistent." *Cronkite News*, https://cronkite-news.azpbs.org/hookedrx/az-pharmacy-stop-opioid-prescription-fraud.

Smith, Phillip. "Big Pharma Has Long Been Accused Of Trying To Block Marijuana Legalization." *AlterNet*, September 9, 2016. www.alternet.org/drugs/maker-deadly-fentanyl-kicks-half-million-dollars-defeat-pot-legalization-arizona.

Travelers Property Casualty Company of America v. Anda, Inc. United States Court of Appeals for the Eleventh Circuit, August 26, 2016. https://casetext.com/case/travelers-prop-cas-co-of-am-v-anda-inc-1.

Volkow, Nora D. "America's Addiction to Opioids: Heroin and Prescription Drug Abuse." *National Institute on Drug Abuse; National Institutes of Health; U.S. Department of Health and Human Services*, May 14, 2014. https://www.drugabuse.gov/about-nida/legislative-activities/testimony-to-congress/2016/americas-addiction-to-opioids-heroin-prescription-drug-abuse.

The White House. "Fact Sheet: Obama Administration Announces Public and Private Sector Efforts to Address Prescription Drug Abuse and Heroin Use." October 21, 2015. https://obamawhitehouse.archives.gov/the-press-office/2015/10/21/fact-sheet-obama-administration-announces-public-and-private-sector.

Ziegler, Annette Kingsland. "Review of *State v. Parisi*." *Supreme Court of Wisconsin*. https://casetext.com/case/state-v-parisi-15.

CHAPTER NOTES

INTRODUCTION

1. Keith Walker, "Introduction." From C. J. Arlotta, *Fighting For A Fix: Reflections Of Mothers Who Lost Children To The Opioid Epidemic* (New York, NY: Forbes Media, 2016), p. 1.
2. "National Center for Health Statistics," *Health: United States: 2015: With Special Feature on Racial and Ethnic Health Disparities* (Hyattsville, MD: U.S. Department of Health and Human Services, CDC. 2016), p. 152. http://www.cdc.gov/nchs /data/hus/hus15.pdf#019.

CHAPTER 1: WHAT THE EXPERTS SAY

1. "Prescription Drug Abuse: What Are Opioids?" *National Institute on Drug Abuse*, November 2014. https://www.drugabuse.gov /publications/research-reports/prescription-drugs/opioids /what-are-opioids.
2. Gabor Maté, "Promo for *In the Realm of Hungry Ghosts: Close Encounters with Addiction*," *Dr. Gabor Maté*, http://drgabormate .com/book/in-the-realm-of-hungry-ghosts.

"OPIOID ADDICTION 2016 FACTS AND FIGURES" BY THE AMERICAN SOCIETY OF ADDICTION MEDICINE

1. National Institute on Drug Abuse. (2015). Drugs of Abuse: Opioids. Bethesda, MD: National Institute on Drug Abuse. Available at http://www.drugabuse.gov/drugs-abuse/opioids.
2. American Society of Addiction Medicine. (2011). Public Policy Statement: Definition of Addiction. Chevy Chase, MD: American Society of Addiction Medicine. Available at http://www .asam.org/docs/publicpolicy-statements/1definition_of_addic- tion_long_4-11.pdf?sfvrsn=2. 3. Center for Behavioral Health Statistics and Quality. (2016). Key substance use and mental health indicators in the United States: Results from the 2015 National Survey on Drug Use and Health (HHS Publication No. SMA 16-4984, NSDUH Series H-51). Retrieved from http:// www.samhsa.gov/data/.
4. National Institute on Drug Abuse. (2014). Drug Facts: Heroin. Bethesda, MD: National Institute on Drug Abuse. Available at http://www.drugabuse.gov/publications/drugfacts/heroin.

5. Centers for Disease Control and Prevention, National Center for Health Statistics. Underlying Cause of Death 1999-2015 on CDC WONDER Online Database, released December, 2016. Data are from the Multiple Cause of Death Files, 1999-2015, as compiled from data provided by the 57 vital statistics jurisdictions through the Vital Statistics Cooperative Program. Accessed at http://wonder.cdc.gov/ucdicd10.html.

6. Paulozzi MD, Jones PharmD, Mack PhD, Rudd MSPH. Vital Signs: Overdoses of Prescription Opioid Pain Relievers – United State, 1999-2008. Division of Unintentional Injury Prevention, National Center for Injury Prevention and Control, Center for Disease Control and Prevention. 2011:60:5.

7. Centers for Disease Control and Prevention. (2014). Opioid Painkiller Prescribing, Where You Live Makes a Difference. Atlanta, GA: Centers for Disease Control and Prevention. Available at http://www.cdc.gov/vitalsigns/opioid-prescribing/.

8. Jones CM. Heroin use and heroin use risk behaviors among nonmedical users of prescription opioid pain relievers - United States, 2002-2004 and 2008-2010. Drug Alcohol Depend. 2013 Sep 1;132(1-2):95-100. doi: 10.1016/j.drugalcdep.2013.01.007. Epub 2013 Feb 12.

9. Cicero TJ, Ellis MS, Surratt HL, Kurtz SP. The changing face of heroin use in the United States: a retrospective analysis of the past 50 years. JAMA Psychiatry. 2014;71(7):821-826.

10. National Institute of Drug Abuse. (2015). Drug Facts: Prescription and Over-the-Counter Medications. Bethesda, MD: National Institute of Drug Abuse. Available at http://www.drugabuse.gov/publications/drugfacts/prescription-over-counter-medications.

11. Fortuna RJ, Robbins BW, Caiola E, Joynt M, Halterman JS. Prescribing of controlled medications to adolescents and young adults in the United States. Pediatrics. 2010;126(6):1108-1116.

12. Center for Disease Control and Prevention. (2013). Prescription Painkiller Overdoses: A Growing Epidemic, Especially Among Women. Atlanta, GA: Centers for Disease Control and Prevention. Available at http://www.cdc.gov/vitalsigns/prescriptionpainkilleroverdoses/index.html.

13. Hedegaard H, Chen LH, Warner M. Drug-poisoning deaths involving heroin: United States, 2000–2013. NCHS data brief, no 190. Hyattsville, MD: National Center for Health Statistics. 2015. Available at http://www.cdc.gov/nchs/data/databriefs/db190.htm.

"AMERICA'S ADDICTION TO OPIOIDS: HEROIN AND PRESCRIPTION DRUG ABUSE" PRESENTED BY NORA D. VOLKOW

[1] UNODC, World Drug Report 2012. http://www.unodc.org/unodc/en/data-and-analysis/WDR-2012.html

[2] Substance Abuse and Mental Health Services Administration, *Results from the 2012 National Survey on Drug Use and Health: Summary of National Findings*, NSDUH Series H-46, HHS Publication No. (SMA) 13-4795. Rockville, MD: Substance Abuse and Mental Health Services Administration, 2013.

[3] Pradip et al. Associations of Nonmedical Pain Reliever Use and Initiation of Heroin Use in the US. Center for behavioral Health Statistics and QualityData Review. SAMHSA (2013) http://www.samhsa.gov/data/2k13/DataReview/DR006/nonmedical-pain-reliever-use-2013.htm

[4] IMS's National Prescription Audit (NPA) & Vector One ®: National (VONA).

[5] International Narcotics Control Board Report 2008.. United Nations Pubns. 2009. p. 20

[6] To clarify our terminology here, when we say "prescription drug abuse" or "nonmedical use," this includes use of medications without a prescription, use for purposes other than for what they were prescribed, or use simply for the experience or feeling the drug can cause.

[7] Substance Abuse and Mental Health Services Administration. Drug Abuse Warning Network, 2007: national estimates of drug-related emergency department visits.

[8] Treatment Episode Data Set (TEDS) Highlights – 2007. National Admissions to Substance Abuse Treatment Services. SAMHSA

[9] Mack, K.A. Drug-induced deaths - United States, 1999-2010. MMWR Surveill Summ. 2013 Nov 22;62 Suppl 3:161-3. CDC

[10] Paulozzi et al. Increasing deaths from opioid analgesics in the United States Pharmacoepidemiol. Drug Saf., 15 (2006), pp. 618–627

[11] Relieving Pain in America: A Blueprint for Transforming Prevention, Care, Education, and Research. REPORT BRIEF JUNE 2011; Johannes et al. The prevalence of chronic pain in United States adults: results of an Internet-based survey. J Pain. 11(11):1230-9. (2010); Gallup-Healthways Well-Being Index.

[12] De Leon Casada. Opioids for Chronic Pain: New Evidence,

New Strategies, Safe Prescribing The American Journal of Medicine, 126(3s1):S3–S11. (2013)..

[13] American Academy of Pain Medicine; American Pain Society; American Society of Addiction Medicine. *Definitions Related to the Use of Opioids for the Treatment of Pain*. Glenview, IL, and Chevy Chase, MD: American Academy of Pain Medicine, American Pain Society, American Society of Addiction Medicine; 2001

[14] Assessment of Analgesic Treatment of Chronic Pain: A Scientific Workshop, linked to 4-24-2014 available at http://www.fda.gov/downloads/Drugs/NewsEvents/UCM308363.pdf

[15] ER/LA Opioid Analgesic Class Labeling Changes and Post-market Requirements (PDF - 136KB) Letter to ER/LA opioid application holders. Linked to 4-24-2014 Available at http://www.fda.gov/downloads/Drugs/DrugSafety/InformationbyDrugClass/UCM367697.pdf

[16] Mattoo, S. Prevalence and correlates of epileptic seizure in substance-abusing subjects. Psychiatry Clin Neurosci. 63(4):580-2. (2009).

[17] SAMHSA: Results from the 2012 National Survey on Drug Use and Health: Summary of National Findings and Detailed Tables

[18] CDC. Vital signs. http://www.cdc.gov/vitalsigns/Prescription-PainkillerOverdoses/index.html

[19] Bateman, B.T. et al. Patterns of Opioid Utilization in Pregnancy in a Large Cohort of Commercial Insurance Beneficiaries in the United States. Anesthesiology. in press (2014)

[20] Coalition Against Insurance Fraud. Prescription for peril: how insurance fraud finances theft and abuse of addictive prescription drugs. Washington, DC: Coalition Against Insurance Fraud; 2007. Available at http://www.insurancefraud.org/downloads/drugDiversion.pdf

[21] Centers for Disease Control and Prevention , National Center for Health Statistics. Multiple Cause of Death 1999-2010 on CDC WONDER Online Database, released 2012. Data are from the Multiple Cause of Death Files, 1999-2010, as compiled from data provided by the 57 vital statistics jurisdictions through the Vital Statistics Cooperative Program.

[22] Substance Abuse and Mental Health Services Administration, Center for Behavioral Health Statistics and Quality. *Treatment Episode Data Set (TEDS): 2001-2011. National Admissions to Substance Abuse Treatment Services*. BHSIS Series S-65, HHS Publication No. (SMA) 13-4772. Rockville, MD: Substance Abuse and Mental Health Services Administration, 2013.

[23] Brody and Li. Am. J. Epidemiology. 2014

[24] Williams, J. Regulation of μ-opioid receptors: desensitization, phosphorylation, internalization, and tolerance. Pharmacol Rev. 65(1):223-54. (2013).

[25] Møller et al. Acute drug-related mortality of people recently released from prisons. Public Health. 124(11):637-9. (2010); Buster et al. An increase in overdose mortality during the first 2 weeks after entering or re-entering methadone treatment in Amsterdam. Addiction. 97(8):993-1001. (2002).

[26] Paulozzi, L. Prescription drug overdoses: a review. J Safety Res. 43(4):283-9 (2012)

[27] CDC.Vital signs: overdoses of prescription opioid pain relievers and other drugs among women--United States, 1999-2010. MMWR 62(26):537-42. (2013).

[28] Slevin and Ashburn. Primary care physician opinion survey on FDA opioid risk evaluation and mitigation strategies. J Opioid Manag. 2011 Mar-Apr;7(2):109-15.

Hooten and Bruce. Beliefs and attitudes about prescribing opioids among healthcare providers seeking continuing medical education. J Opioid Manag. 7(6):417-24.(2011).

[29] Substance Abuse and Mental Health Services Administration, *Results from the 2012 National Survey on Drug Use and Health: Summary of National Findings*, NSDUH Series H-46, HHS Publication No. (SMA) 13-4795. Rockville, MD: Substance Abuse and Mental Health Services Administration, 2013.

[30] SAMHSA advisory Bulletin 2/7/14 http://www.samhsa.gov/newsroom/advisories/1402075426.aspx).

[31] Centers for Disease Control and Prevention , National Center for Health Statistics. Multiple Cause of Death 1999-2010 on CDC WONDER Online Database, released 2012. Data are from the Multiple Cause of Death Files, 1999-2010, as compiled from data provided by the 57 vital statistics jurisdictions through the Vital Statistics Cooperative Program.

[32] Moore, A. et al. Expect analgesic failure; pursue analgesic success BMJ. 3;346 (2013).

[33]Community-Based Opioid Overdose Prevention Programs Providing Naloxone. United States, 2010. U.S. Department of Health and Human Services. Centers for Disease Control and Prevention. MMWR. Vol 61/No.6 February 17, 2012.

[34]NIDA STTR Grantee: AntiOp, Inc., Daniel Wermerling, CEO.

[35] Schwartz, R.P. et al. Opioid agonist treatments and heroin overdose deaths in Baltimore, Maryland, 1995-2009. Am J Public Health. 103(5):917-22 (2013).

[36] Zarkin, G. Benefits and costs of methadone treatment: results

from a lifetime simulation model. Health Econ. 14(11): 1133-50 (2005).

[37] Knudsen, H.K.; Abraham, A.J.; and Roman, P.M. Adoption and implementation of medications in addiction treatment programs. J Addict Med 2011; 5:21-27.

[38] National Institute on Drug Abuse. *Principles of Drug Addiction Treatment: A Research-Based Guide (Third Edition)*, NIH Publication No. 12-4180. Rockville, MD: National Institute on Drug Abuse, 2012. www.drugabuse.gov/publications /principles-drug-addiction-treatment

[39] Spoth et al. Longitudinal substance initiation outcomes for a universal preventive intervention combining family and school programs. *Psychology of Addictive Behaviors* 16(2):129–134, 2002.

[40] teens.drugabuse.gov/peerx.

[41] CDC. Home and Recreational Safety. www.cdc.gov/HomeandRecreationalSafety/overdose/guidelines.html

"FENTANYL LAW ENFORCEMENT SUBMISSIONS AND INCREASES IN SYNTHETIC OPIOID– INVOLVED OVERDOSE DEATHS – 27 STATES, 2013–2014" BY R. MATTHEW GLADDEN

Drug Enforcement Administration. DEA issues nationwide alert on fentanyl as threat to health and public safety. Washington, DC: US Department of Justice, Drug Enforcement Administration; 2015. http://www.dea.gov/divisions/hq/2015/hq031815.shtml

CDC. CDC Health Advisory: Increases in fentanyl drug confiscations and fentanyl-related overdose fatalities. Atlanta, GA: US Department of Health and Human Services, CDC; 2015. http:// emergency.cdc.gov/han/han00384.asp

Drug Enforcement Administration Counterfeit prescription pills containing fentanyls: a global threat. DEA intelligence brief. Washington, DC: US Department of Justice, Drug Enforcement Administration; 2016. https://www.dea.gov/docs/Counterfeit%20Prescription%20Pills.pdf

Drug Enforcement Administration National heroin threat assessment summary—updated. DEA intelligence report. Washington, DC: US Department of Justice, Drug Enforcement Administration; 2016. https://www.dea.gov/divisions/hq/2016 /hq062716_attach.pdf

Peterson AB, Gladden RM, Delcher C, et al. Increases in fentanyl-related overdose deaths—Florida and Ohio, 2013–2015. MMWR Morb Mortal Wkly Rep 2016;65:844–9.

CDC. Reported law enforcement encounters testing positive for fentanyl increase across US. Atlanta, GA: US Department of Health and Human Services, CDC; 2016. http://www.cdc.gov /drugoverdose/data/fentanyl-le-reports.html

National Center for Health Statistics. Percent of drug poisoning deaths that mention the type of drug(s) involved, by state: 2013–2014. Atlanta, GA: US Department of Health and Human Services, CDC, National Center for Health Statistics; 2014. http://www.cdc.gov/nchs/data/health_policy/unspecified _drugs_by_state_2013-2014.pdf

Peng PW, Sandler AN. A review of the use of fentanyl analgesia in the management of acute pain in adults. Anesthesiology 1999;90:576–99. CrossRefPubMed

Hedegaard H, Chen LH, Warner M. Drug-poisoning deaths involving heroin: United States, 2000–2013. NCHS Data Brief 2015;190:1–8. PubMed

US Department of Health and Human Services. Opioid abuse in the U.S. and HHS actions to address opioid-drug related overdoses and deaths. Washington, DC: US Department of Health and Human Services, Office of the Assistant Secretary for Planning and Evaluation; 2015. http://aspe.hhs.gov/sites /default/files/pdf/107956/ib_OpioidInitiative.pdf

* Additional information on approved fentanyl products and their indications is available at http://www.accessdata.fda.gov/scripts/ cder/drugsatfda/index.cfm?fuseaction=Search.SearchAction&- SearchTerm=fentanyl&SearchType=BasicSearch.

† Arkansas, California, Colorado, Connecticut, Florida, Illinois, Iowa, Kentucky, Massachusetts, Maine, Maryland, Minnesota, Missouri, Nevada, New Hampshire, New York, North Carolina, Ohio, Oklahoma, Oregon, Tennessee, Texas, Utah, Virginia, Washington, West Virginia, and Wisconsin.

§ Data were extracted July 1, 2016; additional information on NFLIS is available at http://www.deadiversion.usdoj.gov/nflis/.

¶ http://www.cdc.gov/nchs/nvss/mortality_public_use_data.htm.

** IMS Health's National Prescription Audit is a trademarked product. http://www.imshealth.com/files/web/IMSH%20Insti- tute/NPA_Data_Brief-.pdf.

†† The analysis excluded states whose reporting of any specific drug or drugs involved in an overdose changed by >10% from 2013 to 2014. These states were excluded because drug specific overdose numbers and rates, including the number and rate synthetic

opioid–involved overdose deaths, were expected to change substantially from 2013 to 2014 because of changes in reporting.

§§ 38 states reported specific drugs on ≥70% of drug overdoses in 2013 and 2014, but only 36 of these states experienced changes in drug reporting of <10 percentage points from 2013 to 2014. Among these 36 states, only 30 reported ≥20 synthetic opioid–involved overdose deaths in 2013 and 2014, and 27 of these 30 states had fentanyl submissions in both 2013 and 2014.

¶¶ Reported drug submissions to NFLIS decreased from 1.54 million in 2013 to 1.51 million in 2014 suggesting that the increase in fentanyl submissions was not driven by general increases in drug submissions to NFLIS. https://www.nflis.deadiversio n.usdoj.gov/DesktopModules/ReportDownloads /Reports/NFLIS2014AR.pdf .

*** Six states reported increases of more than two synthetic opioid deaths per 100,000 residents (Kentucky [2.4], Maine [3.0], Maryland [2.2], Massachusetts [5.2], New Hampshire [9.1], and Ohio [3.7]), and seven of the eight states reported increases of ≥100 in synthetic opioid deaths (Florida [143], Kentucky [103], Maryland [137], Massachusetts [355], New Hampshire [121], North Carolina [100], and Ohio [423]).

††† The following reports are from seven of the eight high-burden states: 1) Florida: https://www.fdle.state.fl.us/cms/MEC/ Publications-and-Forms/Documents/Drugs-in-Deceased-Persons/2014-Annual-Drug-Report-FINAL.aspx; 2) Maine: http:// pub.lucidpress.com/NDEWSFentanyl/; 3) Maryland: http:// bha.dhmh.maryland.gov/OVERDOSE_PREVENTION/Documents/2015.05.19%20-%20Annual%20OD%20Report%202014_ merged%20file%20final.pdf; 4) Massachusetts: http://www.mass. gov/eohhs/docs/dph/quality/drugcontrol/county-level-pmp/ data-brief-overdose-deaths-may-2016.pdf; 5) New Hampshire: http://nhpr.org/post/nh-medical-examiner-least-10-drug-overdoses-2016-86-cases-pending, http://mediad.publicbroadcasting.net/p/nhpr/files/201604/drug_data_update_from_nh_medical_examiner_s_office_4-14-16__3_.pdf; 6) Ohio: http://www. medscape.com/viewarticle/851502; and 7) Kentucky: http:// www.mc.uky.edu/kiprc/programs/kdopp/reports/2015-drug-overdose-deaths.pdf. Other jurisdictions also reporting sharp increases in fentanyl deaths include 1) Pennsylvania: https:// www.dea.gov/divisions/phi/2015/phi111715_attach.pdf, https:// www.dea.gov/divisions/phi/2016/phi071216_attach.pdf; 2) New York City: https://a816-health30ssl.nyc.gov/sites/nychan/Lists/ AlertUpdateAdvisoryDocuments/Fentanyl-HAN-advisory.pdf;

and 3) Rhode Island: http://www.slideshare.net/OPUNITE /rx16-federal-tues2001gladden2halpin3green.

§§§ Large fringe metro counties are located in metropolitan statistical areas (MSAs) of ≥1 million population that did not qualify as large central metro counties. Large central metro counties are MSAs of ≥1 million population that 1) contain the entire population of largest principal city of the MSA, 2) have their entire population contained in the largest principal city of the MSA, or 3) contain at least 250,000 inhabitants of any principal city of the MSA.

¶¶¶ http://www.cdc.gov/mmwr/preview/mmwrhtml/mm6450a3.htm.

CHAPTER 2: WHAT THE GOVERNMENT SAYS

1. National Center for Health Statistics, "Highlights," *Health: United State: 2015: With Special Feature on Racial and Ethnic Health Disparities* (Hyattsville, MD: US Department of Health and Human Services, CDC. 2016), p. 4. http://www.cdc.gov /nchs/data/hus/hus15.pdf#019.

CHAPTER 3: WHAT THE COURTS SAY

1. Katie De Rosa, "Fentanyl Crisis: Are Harsher Sentences the Answer?" *Times-Colonist*, October 25, 2016. http://www.times-colonist.com/news/local/fentanyl-crisis-are-harsher-sentences-the-answer-1.2372520.

EXCERPT FROM *STATE OF WISCONSIN V. ANDY J. PARISI* FROM THE SUPREME COURT OF WISCONSIN

1. The Honorable Daniel J. Bissett presided.
2. The facts in this section are taken from testimony provided at the July 12, 2013 suppression hearing.
3. Narcan is the trade or brand name of the narcotic antagonist naxolone. 2 Robert K. Ausman and Dean E. Snyder, <u>Ausman & Snyder's Medical Library: Lawyers Edition</u> § 3:45 (1988). "Naxolone is a narcotic antagonist indicated for the complete or partial reversal of narcotic depression, including respiratory depression, induced by narcotics such as . . . heroin . . . . Naxolone is also indicated for the diagnosis of suspected acute

narcotic overdosage." Id.

4. Counsel for Parisi asked Officer Moua on cross-examination whether each of six specific officers had been present at the residence. Officer Moua confirmed that five out of the six named officers were present, but could not remember whether the sixth named officer had also been present. Officer Moua then volunteered that there had also been a sergeant present at the residence, bringing the potential number of officers at the residence to seven. Yet when counsel for Parisi then asked Officer Moua, in summary, if a total of "possibly five to six officers were involved" in the case, Officer Moua responded, "Sure." Officer Fenhouse similarly testified that there had been between five and six officers involved in the medical call.

5. On direct examination Officer Moua testified that the officers were at the apartment "probably within the hour." On cross-examination counsel for Parisi asked: Q: And when the State asked you how long you-- the officers were on scene, you said within an hour? A: I said probably about an hour, sure. Q: So maybe slightly less than an hour? A: I couldn't even remember.

6. This last fact was taken from the affidavit in support of the criminal complaint against Parisi.

7. All subsequent references to the Wisconsin Statutes are to the 2013-14 version unless otherwise indicated.

8. The defense informed the circuit court, "I guess I would have no objection to the [c]ourt considering the scientific article because I certainly think there's been some peer review of that."

9. As the State clarified on appeal, the Rook article indicates a window of 10 to 40 minutes. Elisabeth J. Rook et al., Pharmacokinetics and Pharmacokinetic Variability of Heroin and its Metabolites: Review of the Literature, 1 Current Clinical Pharmacology 111 (2006).

CONCLUSION

1. Parisi asserts a violation of both the Fourth Amendment to the U.S. Constitution and a violation of Article I, § 11 of the Wisconsin Constitution. When we refer to the Fourth Amendment in this discussion, we intend the discussion to be equally applicable to Article I, § 11 of the Wisconsin Constitution. "Generally, we have interpreted provisions of the Wisconsin Constitution consistent with the United States Supreme Court's interpretation of their counterparts in the federal constitution. However, on occasion, we have interpreted a

provision in the Wisconsin Constitution more broadly than the United States Supreme Court has interpreted a parallel provision in the United States Constitution." State v. Arias, 2008 WI 84, ¶19, 311 Wis. 2d 358, 752 N.W.2d 748 (citations omitted).

2. The majority goes to such lengths to minimize the evidentiary value of morphine in the blood that it does not even bother to determine how long morphine is detectable after heroin use. According to the majority: "We do not possess, but do not require, information regarding precisely how long morphine remains in the human body after ingestion of heroin." Majority op. ¶44 n.14.

   The majority is incorrect. At oral argument, Parisi's counsel explained that according to the Rook article supplied by the State, "the metabolites of heroin stay in the system for 12, could be even 24 hours..."

3. <u>Bohling</u> makes clear that it is specific to the drunk driving context. It stated that "a warrantless blood sample taken at the direction of a law enforcement officer is permissible under the following circumstances: (1) the blood draw is taken to obtain evidence of intoxication from a person lawfully arrested for a <u>drunk-driving related violation or crime</u>, (2) there is a clear indication that the blood draw will produce evidence of intoxication, (3) the method used to take the blood sample is a reasonable one and performed in a reasonable manner, and (4) the arrestee presents no reasonable objection to the blood draw." <u>State v. Bohling</u>, 173 Wis. 2d 529, 533-34, 494 N.W.2d 399 (1993) (emphasis added) abrogated by Missouri v. McNeely, 133 S. Ct. 1552, 185 L. Ed. 2d 696 (2013). The majority opinion fails to accurately state these requirements. It omits the first factor, which provides an essential distinction between <u>Bohling</u> and this case. <u>See</u> majority op. ¶31 & n.11.

4. The majority opinion dismisses the scientific articles Parisi submitted and instead relies on a solo article submitted by the State. <u>See</u> majority op. ¶43 n.13.

5. The majority fails to adequately explain its singular focus of needing to find heroin ——not morphine——in the blood. Parisi was charged with Possession of a Schedule I or II narcotic drug. Wis. Stat. § 961.41(3g)(am) provides that: "If a person possesses or attempts to possess a controlled substance included in schedule I or II which is a narcotic drug... the person is guilty of a Class I felony." Even if the police had only been able to convict Parisi of possession of morphine, both heroin and morphine carry the same criminal penalty. <u>See</u> Wis. Stat. §§ 961.14(3)(k) and 961.16(2)(a)10.

CHAPTER 4: WHAT THE ADVOCATES SAY

1. Emma K. Genco et al., "Clinically Inconsequential Alerts: The Characteristics of Opioid Drug Alerts and Their Utility in Preventing Adverse Drug Events in the Emergency Department," *Annals of Emergency Medicine*, Volume 67, Issue 2, pp. 240 - 248. http://dx.doi.org/10.1016/j.annemergmed.2015.09.020.
2. John Weeks, "Common Sense: Use All Proven Pain Methods in a Comprehensive Strategy to Prevent Opioid Abuse," *The Journal of Alternative and Complementary Medicine*. September 2016, 22(9): 677-679.

"TRENDS IN HEROIN USE IN EUROPE: WHAT DO TREATMENT DEMAND DATA TELL US?" FROM THE EUROPEAN MONITORING CENTRE FOR DRUGS AND DRUG ADDICTION (EMCDDA)

[1] This data set does not include all heroin users entering opioid substitution treatment as in some countries this type of treatment can be provided by office-based medical doctors or other providers that are not covered by the TDI.

[2] The primary drug is defined as "the drug that causes the client the most problems at the start of the treatment. This is usually based on the request made by the clients and (or) on the diagnosis made by a therapist, commonly using international standard instruments (e.g. ICD-10; DSM-IV (5), ASI) or clinical assessment." (EMCDDA, 2012a).

[3] For the division between Western European countries (WECs) and Eastern European countries (EECs), a simple geographical breakdown, considering historical and social factors in the development of the heroin epidemic, has been done (Barrio G., 2013). WECs are Belgium, Denmark, Germany, Ireland, Greece, Spain, France, Italy, Luxembourg, Malta, the Netherlands, Austria, Portugal, Finland, Sweden, the United Kingdom and Norway. EECs are Bulgaria, the Czech Republic, Estonia, Cyprus, Latvia, Lithuania, Hungary, Poland, Romania, Slovenia, Slovakia, Croatia and Turkey. Six countries (Belgium, Estonia, Luxembourg, Hungary, Poland and Norway) did not allow for trend analysis.

[4] Bulgaria, the Czech Republic, Denmark, Germany, Ireland, Greece, Spain, Cyprus, Latvia, the Netherlands, Romania, Slovenia, Finland, Sweden and the United Kingdom.

[5] The annual percentage change (APC) is a measure of the year

on year growth rate and is calculated using log-linear regression. It is used here to characterise the change during a period of time where no joinpoint has been identified. For full details see surveillance.cancer.gov/joinpoint/aapc.html

(⁶) All EU Member States, with the exception of Belgium, Estonia, Luxembourg, Hungary and Poland, plus Croatia and Turkey.

(⁷) The average annual percentage change (AAPC) is a summary measure for a period of time characterised by more than one annual percentage change, i.e. for a period of time during which a joinpoint has been identified. It is calculated as weighted sum of the slope coefficients of the individual regression lines, the weights being the number of years covered by the line segment, transformed into a year on year growth rate. For full details see http://surveillance.cancer.gov/joinpoint/aapc.html#1

(⁸) An important change in reporting method was introduced in UK in 2006 (from paper to electronic reporting).

(⁹) According to some studies, most clients first requested treatment around 2–4 years after starting heroin use (Nordt C.Wiessing , 2010). However, there will also be a few cases with very long time lags of 15, 20 or more years. Given this skewed distribution, the average (mean) time lag will be longer than the time lag of most clients and cannot be used to simply subtract the same number of years from the observed trend in treatment demand to obtain the incidence curve of heroin use in the community. Modelling exercises have also shown that, around the peak of an epidemic of heroin use, one will observe a high number of clients with a very short time lag to treatment, whereas, when an epidemic is declining, fewer cases will be observed but with a longer average time lag between first use and first treatment (e.g. Hickman et al., 2001).

REFERENCES

Barrio, G., Montanari, L., Bravo, M. J., Guarita, B., de la Fuente, L., Pulido, J. and Vicente, J. (2013), 'Trends of heroin use and heroin injection epidemics in Europe: findings from the EMCDDA treatment demand indicator (TDI)', *Journal of Substance Abuse Treatment* 45(1), pp. 19–30.

De la Fuente, L., Brugal, M.T., Domingo-Salvany, A., Bravo, M.J., Neira-León, M. and Barrio, G. (2006), 'More than thirty years of illicit drugs in Spain: a bitter story with some messages for the future', *Revista Española de Salud Pública* (80), pp. 505–20.

EMCDDA (2011), *2011 Annual report on the state of the drugs prob-*

lem in Europe, Publications Office of the European Union, Luxembourg (available at: http://www. emcdda.europa.eu/pub-lications/annual-report/2011).

EMCDDA (2012a), *Treatment demand indicator (TDI), standard protocol 3.0* (available at: http://www.emcdda.europa.eu).

EMCDDA (2012b), '2012 EMCDDA Statistical bulletin' (available at: http://www. emcdda.europa.eu/stats12).

EMCDDA (2012c), *2012 Annual report on the state of the drugs problem in Europe*, Publications Office of the European Union, Luxembourg (available at: http://www. emcdda.europa.eu /publications/annual-report/2012).

Hickman, M., Seaman, S. and Angelis, D. (2001), 'Estimating the relative incidence of heroin use: appplication of a method for adjusting observed reports of first cisits to specialised drug treatment agencies', *American Journal of Epidemiology* 153, pp. 632- 41.

National Cancer Institute (2011), 'Joint Point Regression Programme 3.5.2', (available at: http://surveillance.cancer.gov/joinpoint/).

Nordt, C., Landolt, K. and Stohler, R. (2009), 'Estimating incidence trends in regular heroin use in 26 regions of Switzerland using methadone treatment data', *Substance Abuse Treatment, Prevention, and Policy* 4:14.

Nordt, C., Wiessing, L. (2010), *Calculate the incidence of heroin use in Europe*.

Nordt, C., Wiessing, L. (2010), *Problem heroin use incidence estimation second phase: comparison of two methods in 11 countries /regions*. Final report. Contract code CT.08. EPI.079.1.0.

UNODC (2012), *World drug report 2012*, United Nations Office on Drugs and Crime, Vienna.

EXCERPT FROM THE PRESCRIPTION OPIOID EPIDEMIC: AN EVIDENCE-BASED APPROACH, EDITED BY G. C. ALEXANDER, S. FRATTAROLI, AND A. C. GIELEN

1. CDC Home & Recreational Safety. Prescription Drug Overdose in the United States: Fact Sheet. Available at: http://www.cdc. gov/homeandrecreationalsafety/overdose/facts.html. (Accessed February 3, 2015).

2. U.S. Drug Enforcement Administration / Operations Division / Office of Diversion Control. The Trafficking and Abuse of Prescription Controlled Substances, Legend Drugs and Over the

Counter Products. 2013. Available at: http://www.mbc.ca.gov/About_Us/Meetings/2013/Materials/materials_20130221_rx-2.pdf. (Accessed February 3, 2015).

3. Warner M, Chen L, Makuc D, Anderson R, Miniño A. Drug Poisoning Deaths in the United States, 1980–2008. NCHS Data Brief, no 81. Hyattsville, MD: National Center for Health Statistics; 2011.

4. Centers for Disease Control and Prevention. CDC Multiple Cause of Death Mortality file. 2013. Available at: http://wonder.cdc. gov/mcd.html. (Accessed September 14, 2015).

5. Substance Abuse and Mental Health Services Administration. Results from the 2012 National Survey on Drug Use and Health: Summary of National Findings. 2013, NSDUH Ser. H-46, DHHS Publ. No. SMA 13-4795. Rockville, MD: SAMHSA.

6. Kolodny A, Courtwright DT, Hwang CS, Kreiner P, Eadie JL, Clark TW, Alexander GC. The Prescription Opioid and Heroin Crisis: A Public Health Approach to an Epidemic of Addiction. Annu Rev Public Health. 2015;36:559-574.

EXCERPT FROM "THE OPIOID SURVEY" FROM THE INTERNATIONAL ADHESIONS SOCIETY

1. Wiseman, DM, Petree, T. Reduction of chronic abdominal and pelvic pain, urological and GI symptoms using a wearable device delivering low frequency ultrasound. International Pelvic Pain Society; Chicago, IL. 2012, Abstract 42, Poster 29. (www.kevmed.com/ClinicalData.html). We have established a separate company, KevMed, LLC to market this device.

CHAPTER 5: WHAT THE MEDIA SAY

1. The Editorial Board, "America's Shocking Maternal Deaths," *The New York Times*, September 3, 2016. http://www.nytimes.com/2016/09/04/opinion/sunday/americas-shocking-maternal-deaths.html.

CHAPTER 6: WHAT ORDINARY PEOPLE SAY

1. Chris Hedges, "A World of Hillbilly Heroin: The Hollowing Out of America, Up Close and Personal," *Al Jazeera*, August 28, 2012. http://www.aljazeera.com/indepth/opinion/2012/08/2012827114532948278.html?utm=from_old_mobile.
2. Conor Friedersdorf, "What OxyContin Addicts in West Virginia Tell Us About the War on Drugs," *The Atlantic*, August 23, 2012. http://www.theatlantic.com/politics/archive/2012/08/what-oxycontin-addicts-in-west-virginia-tell-us-about-the-war-on-drugs/261471.
3. C. J. Arlotta, "Preface." *Fighting For A Fix: Reflections Of Mothers Who Lost Children To The Opioid Epidemic* (New York, NY: Forbes Media, 2016).

CONCLUSION

1. Andre Picard, "Opioid Overuse Is Creating 'Lost Generation,' Expert Says," *The Globe and Mail*, September 1, 2016. http://www.theglobeandmail.com/news/national/opioid-overuse-is-creating-lost-generation-expert-says/article31547148.
2. David Wong, "How Half of America Lost its F**king Mind," *Cracked*, October 12, 2016. http://www.cracked.com/blog/6-reasons-trumps-rise-that-no-one-talks-about.
3. Olga Khazan, "Why Are So Many Middle-Aged White Americans Dying?" *The Atlantic*, January 29, 2016. http://www.theatlantic.com/health/archive/2016/01/middle-aged-white-americans-left-behind-and-dying-early/433863.
4. Katie de Rosa, "Fentanyl Crisis: Are Harsher Sentences the Answer?" *Times-Colonist*, October 25, 2016, http://www.times-colonist.com/news/local/fentanyl-crisis-are-harsher-sentences-the-answer-1.2372520.
5. *Team Recovery*, http://www.theteamrecovery.org.

GLOSSARY

chronic—A continuing health condition; chronic pain lasts at least three months.

conscience—Self-awareness; in this context, the ability to choose whether or not to consent to orders from a government authority, based on one's religion and moral beliefs

hepatic—Involving the liver; a drug that is metabolized hepatically is broken down by the body's liver

illicit—Illegal; illicit drugs are bought and sold illegally, instead of being marketed according to laws meant to control these substances and the pharmaceutical industry.

metabolism—The body's process of using food, oxygen, and medications in our cells. When a drug is metabolized, the body's cells have used it up and are clearing away the waste products.

modi operandi—The way things are done; a phrase in Latin meaning "operating methods."

morbidity and mortality—A phrase used by medical professionals discussing ill health and deaths, particularly when discussing how medical treatment is affecting the ill health and deaths of their patients.

overdose—A dose of a drug which is larger or stronger than needed; can cause injury or death. A fatal overdose of opioids will stop a person from breathing, and he or she will die.

palliative—A type of medical care for a person at the end of his or her life, including pain management, often in a hospital or hospice.

pertussis—The virus that causes whooping cough; though preventable by vaccination, this disease has not disappeared and can be fatal, particularly for small children or people with weakened immune systems.

placebo effect—The relief of pain or illness by a useless or pretend treatment such as a sugar pill; believed to be the result of brain neurology but still not understood; distinct from pain relief by alternative treatments but can work in harmony with them. Placebo is Latin for "I please (you)."

rehab—Short for "rehabilitation"; a treatment program to help a person recover from an injury or illness. In this context, a person "going to rehab" is in a residential treatment center, being treated to recover from addiction.

Rx—A traditional abbreviation for prescription.

stigma—A mark of disgrace, or a strong feeling of disapproval by society.

trafficking—Moving illicit products from one person to another, or one place to another; used to describe shipping drugs, selling them, or giving them to people.

FURTHER READING

BOOKS

Adams, Taite. *Opiate Addiction – The Painkiller Addiction Epidemic, Heroin Addiction and the Way Out*. UK: Rapid Response Press, 2013.

Arlotta, C. J. *Fighting for a Fix: Reflections of Mothers Who Lost Children to the Opioid Epidemic*. New York, NY: Forbes Media, 2016.

Pierce, Simon. *Prescription Drugs: Opioids That Kill*. New York, NY: Lucent Press, 2017.

Quinones, Sam. *Dreamland: The True Tale of America's Opiate Epidemic*. New York, NY: Bloomsbury Press, 2016.

WEBSITES

European Monitoring Centre for Drugs and Drug Addiction (EMCDDA)

www.emcdda.europa.eu

The EMCDDA was set up to provide factual, objective, reliable, and comparable information concerning drugs, drug addiction, and their consequences.

National Institute on Drug Abuse (NIDA)

www.drugabuse.gov

NIDA's mission is to advance science on the causes and consequences of drug use and addiction and to apply that knowledge to improve individual and public health.

Public Health Agency of Canada

www.healthycanadians.gc.ca

The Public Health Agency has a website with reliable, easy-to-understand health and safety information for Canadians and health professionals. Enter "opioid" in the Search engine to find hundreds of links to articles from the Canadian health ministry.

INDEX